UNIVERSAL LIFE LESSONS

FROM MY BRILLIANT
BLUE BOHEMIAN
Butterfly

SUSAN BALL

Universal Life Lessons
© Susan Ball 2015

All rights reserved. No part of this publication may be reproduced, stored in a retrieval system, or transmitted in any form or by any means, electronic, mechanical, photocopying, recording or otherwise, without the prior written permission of the author.

National Library of Australia Cataloguing-in-Publication entry (pbk)

Creator:	Ball, Susan, author
Title:	Universal Life Lessons from My Brilliant Blue Bohemian Butterfly / Susan Ball
ISBN:	978-0-9943381-6-7 (paperback)
Subjects:	Paas, Anna Rose Women--Australia--Biography Self help

Dewey Number: 920.72

Published by Susan Ball and InHouse Publishing
www.inhousepublishing.com.au

Printed using Envirocare paper

This book is dedicated to

Anna Rose Paas

ACKNOWLEDGING AND HONOURING HER LIFE
AND SHARING HER UNIVERSAL LIFE LESSONS

Shortly after Anna, my brilliant blue bohemian butterfly, passed away, I penned this poem reflecting on the way she had touched so many people's lives with her own purposeful and mindful character, and charm.

Anna had butterfly wings that gently wove magic into the hearts and souls of many. Her goodness always shone through.

>Yummy sweet nectar that tastes so good
>In colourful flowers that are misunderstood
>As any butterfly knows they are there just for us
>To swoon and to fly and to make fairy dust
>Nectar—abundant and strong
>To build us up and make us feel good
>As any butterfly knows its wonderful food
>And most of all hidden from all to see
>Except for butterflies who are free
>And are ready for the next stage
>When we open our wings and take flight
>As any butterfly knows—it's heaven's delight

Preface

I have, for many years, known that this book needed to be written. Now that Anna is my guardian angel, I feel the strong desire and passion to share this amazing woman's story and for her legacy to live on.

I would like to thank so many people who have their imprint in the ink of this book. They know who they are. It is as though they are all in the words and their souls and spirits are part of the stories woven, like a tapestry, in Universal Life Lessons from *Universal Life Lessons from My Brilliant Blue Bohemian Butterfly*.

So many people have encouraged me to write this book.

Peter Ellyard, author and futurist, who has written many books including *Designing 2050*, has shared many a deep and meaningful conversation with me suggesting that I should write a book about unconditional love 'as you live it every day'. At the time, I didn't know what he meant. I do now.

At the Woodford Festival in 2013 I was given a Body of Consciousness reading. It was a strange thing for me to do as it wasn't the sort of thing I was into at that time. For some reason it felt right so I accepted the offer for a free reading, where they gave me some wonderful advice that I subsequently followed. However, the gem was that when I got home I noticed that she had also put a slip of paper in my bag that read, "You should also write a book as you have the power to heal others." It blew me away.

It was not long after this that I had another profound message sent to me in the shape of two loving sisters who I met one morning in February 2014 when they were walking along Bulcock Beach in Caloundra at sunrise. I had never met them before and they both looked very connected and just by looking at their body language and their features, I took them as sisters. However, I also felt their sadness. They were taking photos of the sunrise and, as I was nearby, I offered to take a photograph of them together. They were appreciative of my offer but declined. Instead they shared with me the recent loss of their mother, who had passed away on Christmas Day. It then became a meaningful exchange and we talked about how to embrace life and how precious it was.

As we parted their words to me were, "You must write a book as you have lifted our spirits with your story of hope and by being so positive." They, too, felt that I had the power to heal through my words and through storytelling. When you hold this book in your hands know that it is filled with love, joy, and the hope that it enables you to bring more meaning into your life through the universal life lessons.

Susan Ball
August 2015

Foreword

Soon after I met Susan Ball I began to feel that she was a person with a special calling. Our conversations over several years confirmed this to me. She often talked about Anna and it was clear to me that Anna's longer-than-expected life, and her amazing relationship with her, was for a higher purpose.

During her life Anna accomplished a heroic journey. Anna was a spectacular presence while she was alive and now she is powerfully moulding Susan's life after she has gone.

Susan experienced what she regards as a privileged twenty-nine years of living with Anna. Through her lenses of unconditional love, she saw Anna as a person with significant abilities and enabled her to live a rich and purposeful life.

Shortly after Anna's passing, Susan commenced writing this marvellous narrative that is meaningful, moving, and beautifully written. During their lives together, Susan became an expert in uplifting the capabilities of people with disability. She is now moving from an expert to an authority through her authoring of what I regard as an authoritative book.

Susan embodies another gift that she brings to her work. She is able to draw rich, generic, and general conclusions from her specific experiences.

Heritage is what we treasure from the past because it is not only important in its own right but also because it informs us of our present actions and how we shape the future.

In this book, Susan reveals Anna's rich heritage. It will inform the work Susan will accomplish during the rest of her life.

Thank you, Anna and Susan, for what has been, and for what is to come.

Peter Ellyard
Author and Futurist
August 2015

Contents

Preface		v
Foreword		vii
Introduction		1
Chapter 1	In the Beginning	3
Chapter 2	Strengthening and Enabling	15
Chapter 3	Connecting	27
Chapter 4	Community Building (UK)	41
Chapter 5	Community Building (Italy)	63
Chapter 6	Transitioning (Australia)	85
Chapter 7	Medical Learnings	103
Chapter 8	Life-Changing Decisions	131
Chapter 9	Honouring	149
Chapter 10	Reflecting	171
Learnings	Universal Life Lessons	193
Glossary		199
Resources		203
Afterword		207
About the Author		209

Introduction

This book brings to life the remarkable legacy of a woman, Anna Rose Paas, who through her determination, courage, and joy of life, touched people's hearts and enabled them to find inner peace and love. Her purpose was to make a difference to this world and she did.

The stories woven into *Universal Life Lessons from My Brilliant Blue Bohemian Butterfly* give hope to everyone that their wishes for a good quality of life can be honoured, from birth through to death, regardless of their circumstances. It is the gift of these valuable lessons that Anna left for all to see and to embrace.

Anna had a very rare condition—Ring 22 Chromosome Abnormality—which meant she was a child in her cognitive development, however in her emotional and spiritual development she was a saint. Anna passed away on 16 April 2015 at the age of twenty-nine years. She defied the odds and lived far beyond her life expectancy with her condition. What she brought to the world in her short life was profound.

It is my honour and privilege as her mother to share her amazing story with you when my heart is filled with pride and peace to know that Anna, now my guardian angel, can still make a difference to others. As our birthdays are exactly thirty years apart, someone who didn't know Anna but had heard about her observed, "Your life has been positively synchronised with a twin." He put another piece of the jigsaw puzzle together— we were, in fact, so connected on so many levels. Anna didn't reach her 30th birthday, however there will be a dual celebration in October this year when I also reach a milestone—double the age of Anna. It will be for the two of us.

I trust you will find that the eighty-five universal life lessons from my brilliant blue bohemian butterfly will provide you with clarity on your journey. Eighty-five is symbolic as Anna was born in 1985. It is yet another piece of the jigsaw puzzle fitting into its rightful place.

You will know which lessons are right for you to embrace at any given time as you progress through your life. Reflect on them, and where they touch your heart; apply them in your day-to-day life. You may even find that by opening the book and finding where it falls open, you can embrace that lesson for the day. If you wish to expand your knowledge and have further growth, my customised workshops are available, which will awaken and enlighten you. Individual Information, Advice, and Guidance sessions are also recommended.

If the universal life lessons change one person's life, then this book has served its higher purpose.

Chapter 1
In the Beginning

What life deals us, and how we handle it, remains firmly in our own hands. Often, we feel helpless or paralysed when something is just too hard. However, whilst being our greatest challenge, how we cope can also be our greatest strength.

What do you do when you are told by a geneticist, "Your child will be a vegetable and will not be able to walk or talk," followed by, "would you like to put her in a home?"

Those words echoed in my ears long after my youngest daughter, Anna, was diagnosed with Ring 22 Chromosome Abnormality one month prior to her second birthday. At that time Anna was still not acknowledging any awareness and was living very much in her own personal 'inner world'. Our family were told to accept her autistic state and to come to terms with it. It was as though the world had turned upside down. I felt myself being very sad and depressed for several months. The reason for this was that we had been given no hope.

After this period of feeling helpless and paralysed, I decided that it was time to change my mindset as it wasn't healthy and certainly wasn't going to improve the situation. It was then that I decided I wanted to enable Anna to reach her full potential and lead a happy and fulfilling life. That was the best decision I ever made. It was life-changing and it brought an inner strength, determination, and joy to us both and to our family. In fact, that decision enabled Anna to start her own courageous and remarkable journey.

Other than the fact that at birth there was no eye contact and that she slept a lot and had floppy muscles, it would not have been evident that there was anything different about Anna except that I had an intuitive voice that kept nagging at me that something wasn't right. I had Leboyer births—natural childbirths where you have no pain relief, in an environment with soft lighting and gentle music, where the baby is placed on your tummy before being immersed in a warm bath where you can bond with them—for both Claire and Anna. I noticed that unlike after Claire's birth, Anna did not gaze into my eyes at all, nor did she when I breastfed her. Also when I carried Anna she would cry unless I held her face down, which made it look like I was carrying a sack of potatoes.

However, rather than ignore my maternal instincts, I set about asking for a referral to a geneticist so that I could confirm if my suspicions were right and, if so, what I could do about it. It was much to my surprise that the result came back that Anna had a very rare condition, with only thirty known cases in the world. Certainly living to adulthood was unlikely. The geneticist said it was a 'rare occurrence'. Nonetheless, it was a huge shock to hear the prognosis and to accept the news that our youngest daughter had this condition that we had never heard of and we just wondered why.

Our life took on a whole different path then as we tried to find ways to improve Anna's quality of life. It was also the start of an appreciation of small steps and small signs that gave us the hope that Anna was improving. With this came great excitement at any advance. It is amazing how grateful you are when those miracles start happening and that is what kept us going. Every time there was a milestone it was celebrated.

> *Lesson 1: Be grateful for small steps and celebrate them with all your heart*

Life throws many things at us, however even in times of adversity there can be many beautiful moments. One such memory I have is when trying desperately to find the CAT scan, after eighteen years, that was originally taken at the hospital where Anna was diagnosed. You can imagine what I was told. The scan was in the archives in the bowels of the hospital and there was no capacity for any of the staff to look for it. I had this thought that maybe, just maybe, the geneticist that Anna had seen when she was under two years old may still be at the hospital and that he might be able to help me find the elusive scan. I was told that he had only just retired the previous week, so I left my name and phone number. I asked if they would give him my details and mention my daughter's name to him as she had defied all the odds and was still alive. This was when we desperately needed his help. It was a long shot.

Much to my amazement, the next day he called. He had remembered Anna due to her rare condition and he was astonished to hear that she was, in fact, still alive. I then explained that our family had focused on Anna the person, not Anna with the medical condition and that subsequently she'd had a wonderful life filled with fun, joy, and love as well as being a globetrotter. That surprised him even more. Fortunately, our hopelessness was short-lived. I said to him, "You can make a difference to Anna's quality of life now by finding the original scan." I could hear from his voice that he was emotional. It may have been that he was feeling guilty, too, hearing that he had not given us hope, when in fact it was the very thing we needed to hear when Anna was diagnosed. There was also a very determined mother pleading with him to make a difference now. Miraculously he agreed to try and find the scan. A week later he phoned me very excitedly to tell me that he had found it. I was so grateful and so relieved.

We met up at a café and it felt very strange, after all those years, seeing him again in person. He looked gleeful and proud of himself. He handed me the 1986 scan as though it was a fragile piece of artwork, knowing how important it was to me. We both had tears in our eyes. He expressed his regret that he had given us no hope. He had honestly thought that Anna's life, according to the thirty known cases in the world at the time, would be difficult and that it was unlikely that she would survive through early childhood. He thought it equally unlikely that she would walk or talk. He was thrilled to hear that Anna had surpassed all expectations. He also hoped that finding the scan would make a difference to Anna and her outcome. Now we shared a common bond—our desire to improve Anna's quality of life.

> **Lesson 2: Reach out to the people you need on your journey**

I never saw him again. The scan was a precious gift that enabled a specialist to compare the two images so that they could see how much Anna's brain had changed since 1986. It was crucial to their findings.

However, what I realised was that it wasn't about finding the scan, although that was very important. It was about closure. The anger that I'd had in me for all those years was gone. Instead I smiled to think we had both been healed.

Now, as I live my life, I fully appreciate those moments that bring such renewed hope and joy. Often it comes from the most unexpected places. Nurture it and celebrate it as those moments can easily be lost without trace. Let them shine through; recognise them and trust in them.

> **Lesson 3: Trust in unexpected moments that bring hope and joy**

Anna's Storybook was written to share her story in order for those who did not know her well to appreciate her character, special qualities, and her uniqueness. It expressed her wishes, her likes, her dislikes, and what made her happy. It was a tool that gave the people, who came into Anna's life, more confidence to connect with her, with a greater understanding of who she was and how they could communicate with her and enjoy her company.

The storybook was written in a person-centred, strengths-based way from Anna's perspective, highlighting her personality and passions. The following excerpt from her storybook gives an insight into Anna's early years and what, I believe, enabled Anna to lead the full life she led as a valued citizen:

> I would like to tell you about some of the things I've done to make me as strong as I am. When I was very little and Mum found out that I needed some help, I went down to Victoria with my family. I was two-and-a-half when we left. I did lots of things like crawling, climbing, jumping and trampolining to strengthen my floppy muscles. During this time, my family also started communicating with me using Makaton sign language, although I took a long time to catch on. At the age of five, I was not as frustrated as I could ask for things like food and drink through signing and words.

Lesson 4: Person-centred storybooks are valuable tools and enablers

The Early Intervention Program made a significant difference to Anna's quality of life. As there was no funding available in Queensland for 1:1 support at that time, our family moved to Geelong, Victoria where we were blessed to have funding approved for an aide for Anna who could work alongside her, and our family, to enable her to have occupational therapy and physiotherapy while integrating those therapies into Anna's early development years when she attended the North Geelong Kindergarten and the North Geelong Pre-school.

This was a significant turning point for her. I remember Anna becoming even more determined for her future. Although Anna was given no hope when she was diagnosed with Ring Chromosome 22, which is a very rare disorder caused by the breaking of chromosome 22 at each of its ends and then reconnecting to form a ring, she was making remarkable progress. Her progression from the autistic state to a beautiful, happy little girl was nothing short of a miracle and credit must go to the many devoted professionals that gave tirelessly to Anna's development.

It was the implementation of the following plan that enabled Anna to be supported and to maintain her health, to strengthen and develop her gross and fine motor skills, and to improve her communication.

Plan 1

Date of Plan: 31/7/1989
Anna's age: 3.9 years

The plan was divided into five areas of development or 'life activities':
1. Living situation
2. Family support
3. Health
4. Development of (a) gross motor (b) fine motor (c) communication (d) social skills
5. Children's program

The plan covered each of the above life areas and focused on Anna's current situation, the goals, the strategies to achieve them, and the person responsible for each particular strategy. Current goals at that time for Anna's development were:

- Good health to be maintained—
  review paediatrician
- Vision to be monitored—
  review ophthalmologist
- Continue improving communication skills—
  review speech therapist
- Opportunity to develop social skills—
  increase pre-school sessions

Plan 2

Date of Plan: 27/7/1990
Anna's age: 4.9 years

This plan was written twelve months after the first one. It was enlightening and very encouraging to see Anna's progression, which was being monitored. A second plan was then developed and individually planned, with similar goals and with a similar supportive team. The format of this plan was identical to Plan 1.

Some plan goals had been achieved and others were progressing well. New goals were set in relation to Anna's increased development, which included:

- Anna's excellent health was to be maintained
- To further extend Anna's gross motor skills
- To continue refining Anna's grasp— fine motor skills
- To increase Anna's communication skills
- Toilet training goals
- To continue to develop her cognitive skills
- To increase her pre-school attendance

From the previous year's planning there were significant advances and increased development in all areas of Anna's life. The devoted support of many professionals, and our family, who supported the program, enabled new goals and accomplishments to be worked towards and achieved.

It was also at about this time that our family separated. Anna's father continued to be integral to Anna's development during these important years and continued to show his love, support and commitment to Anna's progression throughout her life.

We were all excited to see Anna's improvement and to see her confidence growing. Her favourite hobby was trampolining, which was introduced in the Early Intervention Program. Trampolining strengthened her core muscles. As far as Anna was concerned it was just downright fun. She developed some funny techniques that truly made you laugh. There were times when we thought that she was going to bounce straight off the trampoline with the amount of gusto she was putting into squats—and cross-legged ones at that! She had mastered the art of trampolining. It gave her so much joy, too.

I'm totally convinced that it was Anna's early intervention focusing on strengthening her core muscles that made her robust and strong, and enhanced her overall wellness and longevity.

Lesson 5: Strengthening core muscles at an early age is very important

There was no doubt that the strengthening of her core muscles greatly assisted Anna in many respects that stood Anna in good stead. There was no such thing in Anna's world called 'occupational therapy'—that word did not exist in her vocabulary. She was simply jumping up and down, enjoying herself. Sometimes she would jump for hours, smiling and saying, "Look at Anna!" which was very endearing. It was the first thing her stepfather saw when he first met her. He met Anna many years later in Brisbane when she was still showing her trampolining skills off proudly. It was very amusing as Anna was singing out loudly "Good girl Anna!" while jumping wildly up and down, smiling, and clapping her hands.

As Colin watched Anna's antics he became even more impressed as she accelerated everything, showing her true mastery of trampolining, clapping, smiling, and talking simultaneously. I was truly surprised and relieved that she didn't go flying into the nearby bushes because I had never seen her perform like that before. Colin was most impressed and was not aware that he had been given such a special performance. He recalls clearly:

> When I first met Anna late in 1994, she was nine years old and enjoying herself on her trampoline—a standard-sized one that her mother had bought her. It was in the garden in her backyard of their house in the inner-Western suburbs of Brisbane. Anna was bouncing up and down from alarmingly high levels as well as doing elementary tricks. She was wearing her school uniform of dark blue shorts and a light blue shirt and she simply exuded joy and confidence.

Lesson 6: Make learning fun and engaging

In view of her love of trampolining, Anna was given a brand new trampoline for her 11th birthday. She used it one day and then refused to ever use it again. That was the end of the trampolining after eight years of daily training—or, to Anna, good old-fashioned fun and jumping up and down! It was exceptional in anyone's eyes that she maintained her love of trampolining for all those years and then stopped so suddenly, but clearly she loved the old one she had, which she had worn out with her tricks and daily routines.

Anna was quite sure at this point in her life that she was not wishing to continue her favourite pastime, so the brand new trampoline was given to our neighbours, who loved it. Maybe that is what she wanted after all!

Fortunately, many years later she resumed her love of trampolining in the UK.

Lesson 7: An early intervention program is beneficial for development and wellness

Chapter 2
Strengthening and Enabling

When someone is not able to tell you that they are hot or cold or, for that matter, hungry, how do you know how to give them the right level of support? After all, we are brought up to understand that when babies cry they are either requiring a change, they need a cuddle, or they're hungry. You very quickly identify which cry is which and how you respond to it. If those signals aren't there and the baby sleeps and has to be woken to eat—and even then you're not sure if they want to be fed, after all you just woke them up from a deep sleep and they seemed perfectly happy without your intervention—it's very difficult to know what to do.

Then take it a step further. What happens when the person is no longer a baby but a young child who is not able to tell you what they want? Basically, they get frustrated and angry at you for not understanding them.

During those early years, we were told that many children with autistic tendencies have behavioural problems. In my opinion, it is more likely that it is simply that the child does not have the tools to express themselves in a way that makes their wishes known.

I recall, vividly, Anna getting very angry when she just couldn't express herself as she had no speech and she was getting more aggressive. It was then that I realised that she needed to learn sign language so that she could show me, and others, another way to understand her.

Lesson 8: Anger and aggressive behaviour might be frustration—signing can assist

As highlighted in *Anna's Storybook,* she was five years old before she said any words at all, and her sister Claire was the honoured one to have heard them come out of her mouth when she was on her beloved rocking horse Star. And yet, Anna started learning Makaton from two-and-a-half years of age. It requires hope and patience and belief that the signing will eventually make a difference. In Anna's case it did. In those formative years, Anna learnt Makaton and so did her family, her friends, and the staff and children at the kindergarten and pre-school.

In a short time Anna began using the signs for eating, drinking, and toileting. She was no longer frustrated and she continued to learn new signs and, as she progressed, we could see her becoming happier and more content. It was also endearing to watch the children so lovingly talk to Anna using the Makaton sign language.

They embraced it. I remember when they had a pair of rabbits in a hutch in the garden. All the children would run over to Anna and do the bunny ears sign and take her by the hand to the hutch and give her some food to give them. I often wondered if having two bunnies was a good idea, as soon the whole of Geelong, where they had been trying to reduce the number of rabbits in the nearby hills, would be over-run by them. But they were cute, white, and had pink noses. So clearly these were very pure rabbits that ate food and were dearly loved by the children, who remained simply oblivious to any such matters.

What was also instructive was that the children at the mainstream kindergarten and pre-school did not find it unusual that they were signing. For them it was another form of play and communication. They didn't see Anna as different either. They saw her as their friend. It was so important, again, in those early years for Anna to feel supported and to enjoy the normal things that other kids did. As a result, Anna, I'm sure, never saw herself as different. She saw herself as a confident, determined person with a great sense of humour and a willingness to take challenges head on.

Lesson 9: See the person, not the disability

After Anna's Early Intervention Program in Geelong we then returned to Brisbane when Anna was five-and-a-half years old. During this time Anna was fortunate to have a case study carried out by students at the Queensland Institute of Technology, focusing on her early development and, in particular, her exceptionality.

They were looking for a child to study and work with in the area of 'exceptionality and young children' and, in their words, they focused on a beautiful young child whose name was Anna. Their comprehensive involvement with Anna, and her very important and significant others who were a major part of her life, enabled them to produce what they described as 'an extremely beneficial and growing time in their careers as early childhood educators'.

ANNA'S AGE:	5.8 years
DOB:	18/10/1985
SEX:	Female
DIAGNOSIS:	Abnormal Karyotype 46, xxr22, a ring chromosome 22 detection
MAJOR DISABILITY:	Ring Chromosome 22
DESCRIPTION OF CHILD:	Anna is a beautiful-looking, healthy, and energetic child. She displays normal growth patterns for her age.

They noted that Anna was introduced to Makaton sign language to assist and facilitate her expressive and receptive communication from an early age. Makaton is divided into various stages of development, starting with first words typical to children's learning of speech. The Makaton language system contains many gestures that closely resemble concepts of words. As a result, those gestures are easy to learn.

Research has shown that a focus on gestural communication will not inhibit acquisition of verbal communication but will instead facilitate speech development because it provides a 'stepping stone' toward comprehension and production of speech. This was very clearly seen in Anna's development.

They also noted in their report that 'a very recent and enormous communication development is that Anna is now not only proficiently using many signs but she is also using the language associated with them'. A very clear example they gave was how Anna used the sign for 'STOP!' while using verbal communication for the word 'stop'.

In their report they commended the teaching team at the childcare centre, who were clearly aware of the benefits of working with a child as special as Anna. Together they strived to incorporate Anna into the daily program and did this, we feel, exceptionally well. The teachers all spoke of Anna first and foremost as an individual, just like each of the other children at the centre. They looked strongly to integrating Anna as 'one of the children' in the group and encouraged her and supported her in every way to participate like every other child.

Lesson 10: Inclusion at an early age, and with support, is extremely important

To cater for her individual developmental levels, the teachers provided, for example:

- More suitable jigsaw puzzles (with pegs on the pieces) to help develop her fine motor skills
- Guidance when using eating utensils
- Time for one-to-one with her
- Support in her toilet training attempts
- Extra time for movement activities outside

They observed that Anna was constantly overcoming everyday challenges. They noted her short attention span. She was always busy and constantly on the move from one activity to the next and needed guidance, at times, to encourage her to finish jigsaws and other activities throughout the day.

Anna often utilised imitation and modelling of other children during her learning. "Pupils can learn from and be supported by one another. Pupils are a resource." (Ainscow and Tweddle, 1988) Eileen Allen further supports this, saying, "Exceptional children can learn through observing and imitating their more able playmates." (Allen, 1980)

They also noticed that Anna experienced frustration, at times, at not being able to communicate easily with other children and adults.

Anna's fine motor skills were also limited, but these skills were being developed by extra materials in the centre, for example jigsaws.

Behaviourally, it was noted that Anna became frustrated at times when she was not able to do something or to communicate adequately. She had difficulty expressing herself to other children but they observed, much to their delight, the devotion and understanding that the other children offered her.

The teachers involved in Anna's program spoke of her being rough at times with them and other children. This was seen in times of frustration and communication difficulties were decreasing.

The children at the centre showed encouragement and enjoyed sharing their time with Anna. The students' overwhelming impression of Anna's day at the childcare centre was that she was an integral part of the centre. Her behavioural problems weren't often displayed due to the positive atmosphere.

They acknowledged and congratulated the teachers at the centre, in conjunction with our family, for the benefits Anna received in the setting. They were humbled by the experience and expressed their gratitude for being able to see such a positive and beneficial program.

In their conclusion they wrote:

> Our personal Early Childhood philosophies have grown and developed immensely in advocating positive attitudes and the belief in the benefits to all who are involved in integrating special children in their programs. Much confidence has been gained in developing, implementing and monitoring the progress of meaningful educational experiences that enhance the

learning of special children. A very important realisation, evident through the research, observation and writing of this paper is that the special child we have chosen to observe was only one of the parties for the children, teachers, adults and every other person who touched Anna's life made a difference.

From the educational perspective, it remains up to the early childhood teachers as to how much everyone's lives will benefit. With the teacher support the benefits are infinite and extremely rewarding.

"When the educational philosophers step down from their platforms and the applause fades away, it remains for you, the teachers, to implement the reforms."
—Dewey, 1980

Lesson 11: Capture the evidence of your child's development

It was fascinating for me to learn, many years later, that sign language can, in fact, not only help with the person to express themselves more easily but also encourages speech to occur, even if it is one word or a sentence at a time. It makes sense when you think about it. The child is more relaxed and they're communicating and expressing themselves through signing. It then enables them, in most cases, to speak when they're ready. It may take some time but it's worth it. Persevere. And if you know someone who is experiencing behavioural problems with their child, if they are not able to express what they want, suggest to them to try signing as it may ease their child's frustration and improve their quality of life.

It is amazing how both the Early Intervention Program and the Early Childhood Program (including Makaton) made a huge difference. I truly believe it was the secret to Anna's start to a full and happy life. Knowing that very few people had lived with her condition to adulthood means that Anna certainly had determination but she also had tools that, throughout her journey, enabled her to build her strength and stamina. We all know that those two qualities are powerful motivators and are extremely important to get through life—even at the toughest of times.

> *Lesson 12: Provide the tools throughout a child's journey to enable growth and development*

> *"Regular children learn about those different from themselves and have the opportunity to learn that the differences are unimportant."*
> —Lewis and Doorlag, 1987

There was no doubt that Anna's peers readily accepted Anna's uniqueness and they helped and guided her in many aspects of her day. The teachers talked excitedly of how the children continually commented on even the smallest achievement she attained.

> *"While teachers are helping special children adjust to a normal environment, they are also educating the other children to see them as feeling, fellow humans."*
>
> —Dewey, 1980

The other learning from those early years of Anna's development was that she was confident. This, in the student's view, was a result of a combination of the love and support from her family and integration at a very early age with children in the kindergarten, pre-school, and childcare centre. It was important to Anna that she was accepted, included, and most of all, valued in all these settings. It showed every day that she was happy.

The case study reinforced my view that once you focus on those three powerful words—accepted, included, and valued—you are empowered and disability pales into insignificance. Anna was different but the same as the other kids. If she saw it that way, why couldn't we? The children who played with her understood this naturally, as they were exposed at any early age to difference and were totally at ease with it. It was mutually rewarding.

In my view, it is this fundamental lesson that is the key to inclusion and achieving the goals of a diverse, rich community.

Lesson 13: Accept, include, and value each person and celebrate their differences

I'm convinced that Anna during her whole life never once thought she had a disability. Like the words 'occupational therapy', the word 'disability' did not exist in Anna's world. Anna was always a child at heart, but even in her late twenties her greatest gift was teaching others how to embrace life and be non-judgmental. She touched people's very souls through her purity.

Every child is exceptional in that he or she is unique. Children, in their uniqueness, differ in levels and quality of development. Diverse and flexible educational opportunities, where each child can feel comfortable within a program, should enable them to reach their full potential. Exceptional children have the same basic needs as other children, other than requiring more support in specific ways. These very special children provide a challenging opportunity and an ultimately rewarding and fulfilling personal satisfaction for early childhood educators.

The more we can embrace difference, the more our society will benefit as a whole and we will achieve so much more together. After all, it's the people's lives we touch that makes a difference to our time on Earth, not how much we have or how many material things we own. They can be taken away from us in an instant and you can't take them with you when you leave. Heartfelt memories of special connections and bonds are with us forever and often enable us to grow and become more compassionate and caring human beings.

If it wasn't for Anna, I don't believe I would be the person I am today. I have been so blessed. This amazing journey has enabled me to understand so many life lessons that I would not have learned otherwise. That is why this storytelling is so important. It needs to be shared while the light is burning bright and I feel the words pouring out of my fingers through the keyboard, just wanting the story to be written. It's as though my higher purpose has been defined by sharing these eighty-five valuable universal life lessons that my brilliant blue bohemian butterfly came to this Earth to share. I feel her with me now, giving me the wings to fly and the belief that it will make a difference. I know that's what she would have wanted.

Lesson 14: Embrace exceptionality and uniqueness, we are all the same but different

Chapter 3
Connecting

Anna, throughout her whole amazing journey, had butterfly wings that touched so many people's hearts. She seemed to be on this Earth to bring goodness and love and to connect with people who may not otherwise have been approachable to a complete stranger. Anna had the magic.

What was it that she had? Whatever it was, she had it in abundance. It was powerful.

I remember that I was unchaining my bicycle recently and getting ready to leave New Farm Park and head home when I heard a couple talking. They were commenting that where I had chained my bike was quite clever as it was away from the maddening crowds at the Italian Festival, tucked discretely away, but still close enough to all the action. I thought it was a good spot too as I hadn't used that area before—there were so many people present that I just found it the easiest place to park it at that time. As I turned around, they acknowledged me. I recognised the lady's face. I was trying to place her but I wasn't able to remember, so fortunately she helped me.

She reminded me that her family had owned a furniture store in Newmarket and that she recalled when Anna and I would come in and buy furniture for our unit up at Caloundra. The first question she asked me was, "How is your gorgeous daughter?"

It was over twenty years since I had last seen her. The fact that she remembered me and, more importantly, had remembered Anna, touched my soul. She talked for ages about how she loved it when we came into their shop as we were always so bright and happy. Her husband then spoke humbly of his recollection of our visits and that it affected him profoundly as he saw such purity in Anna and he was touched by our very strong bond. I was so moved that we had connected with them on a level deeper than I had ever imagined. It is amazing what people see that you don't. At the time I simply knew that Anna and I were just hanging out and ordering furniture, when in fact we were touching people's hearts.

I suppose it could be that Anna was always a six-year-old child developmentally throughout her life. This brought purity, combined with her beautiful soul, which was an elixir that for anyone wanting to taste it drew them in and made them a little tipsy from the experience. That's what I saw time and time again. It was so infectious.

Lesson 15: Inner joy and connecting in heart space is contagious—spread the love

I also saw a wicked side to Anna's sense of humour. She also had an astute wisdom. She would know instinctively when to act dumb around the people that thought she was and to rise above the expectations of those people who believed in her. It was wonderful to watch those times when she extended beyond her comfort zone and was given the opportunity to demonstrate her exceptionality. It all depended on the people around her as to which Anna she would be at any given time. It was funny one evening when we were having a birthday party for Anna's older sister, Claire, who was always a wonderful support throughout Anna's life. We had invited all their cousins, aunties, and uncles to the celebration. It was a lovely evening with many relatives who had not seen each other for a long time. Anna had an uncanny way of saying 'Dad' to her uncle, who was an identical twin, and that night was no exception.

Just before bed time, Anna went around saying 'this one' then kissing everyone good night, so it took a while for her to do the rounds of all the guests. When she came to her Uncle John, she was asked the question, "Anna, if this is your Dad [pointing to Anna's father who stood opposite his identical twin brother] then who is this?" Everyone was quiet, waiting for Anna to respond, as she had a cheeky grin that everyone could see was very mischievous. She looked from one to the other and then, when all the eyes were on her, she said with great clarity and conviction, "Santa!" It was hilarious as both men had white beards. Everyone burst into laughter and could see that Anna had quite a sophisticated sense of humour, which she camouflaged well, unless she had a captive audience in front of whom she could perform. That night she did it beautifully and with great aplomb.

Lesson 16: Encourage laughter and a sense of humour

Reaching our fullest potential is often forgotten in our view of life. I'm not sure why as it really is what we should all aim for, no matter what our circumstances or what life deals us. The way to lead our lives and make them 'well-lived', leaving a legacy behind us, is to be mindful of others and to let them shine. It was my mindset from when Anna had her diagnosis, and I had a chance to reflect, that I would focus on Anna achieving her fullest potential and to have no expectations of how that might look.

Celebrating those special moments, like her first words, her first steps, seeing her smile and then seeing her wicked sense of humour emerge—those moments were precious.

Connecting with others and making a life-changing impact on them was also a quality that Anna had, wherever we were. We could be out shopping, where Anna would gleefully grab the shopping trolley and robustly aim it for the first aisle, intent on finding the items scribbled in a circle that would represent the milk, bread, butter, and other items on her shopping list. As we had always had the conversation prior to the shopping excursion, Anna knew what we needed so she focused intently on the task with great gusto. Many customers often nearly got side-swiped or run over by Anna's trolley, but somehow they suddenly became part of the experience. They mostly joined in the fun and asked her what her name was, which often meant a slight detour from her mission of finding that elusive loaf of bread, and she would reply with equally great excitement and loudness 'Anna' as though she expected them to know who she was. After that, they certainly did. Often I would see smiles and comments as she returned resolutely to her mission.

After each aisle was 'done', as Anna would call it, the highlight was her placing—and I might add, not gently—all the items at the checkout. That was entertaining in itself and would usually mean at least three or four people chatting with her and wanting to know more about her. She was busy. Very busy. She concentrated while moving the groceries from the trolley onto the moving counter. Then, if they survived that process, she would pack them into their respective bags. I never let her have the eggs as I knew they wouldn't stand a chance! So there was a little bit of overseeing to be done here, as a safeguard for Anna and the other customers' safety, and of course, saving the fragile eggs from harm's way.

Then we would have a coffee or a milkshake. And again, there was a hardly a time went by when we weren't joined by someone happy to see us basking in the glory of a job well done after the shopping mission had been accomplished.

Something as ordinary as shopping became extraordinary. It was like Anna and I when we were together were like a magnet drawing the world to us. We had absolutely no agenda, no judgement, and no heavy conversation. We simply lived each moment as if it were a precious gem. And it was.

Lesson 17: Be mindful of others—let them shine

After Anna had reached school age and finished at her pre-school she commenced her schooling at Mitchelton Special State School. It was a difficult decision knowing whether, after receiving mainstream education during her kindergarten and pre-school years, a special school was the best option.

We believe it was the right one for Anna as the mainstream schools did not have funding at that time for teachers' aides and she would not therefore have received the support she needed to excel.

Before Anna enrolled there was a lot of preparation to make sure it was the right school for her. I can honestly put hand to heart and say that the school was absolutely right for her needs.

There is no right or wrong decision. You do your best at any given time and make informed decisions. By continuing to trust in our decisions and always doing our due diligence, we felt confident that the path we had chosen for Anna would improve her quality of life and give her the best opportunity of reaching her full potential.

Lesson 18: Due diligence and trusting in your decisions gives you strength

During this period, Anna's love for trampolining continued and it was part of her routine when she came home on the school bus. She would then have afternoon tea and jump to her heart's content until she couldn't jump anymore.

Independence was one of the main goals that Anna had in her Individual Goals Plan. Independence covered things like travelling on the school bus with her friends to and from school, which she loved. It was one of the highlights of her day.

It also covered toilet timing and personal hygiene. This routine we continued at home so that there was consistency in both her school and home environments.

There was also the goal of improving her communication, which was so important after her Early Intervention Program had been so effective. We wanted to build on that. We continued to use Makaton sign language and incorporated pictures of daily tasks like swimming, trampolining, and going for a drive. She became familiar with them and would choose which activity she would like to do by selecting the relevant picture. It was another very effective tool to improve her communication.

Her writing skills were limited due to her condition, which affected her fine motor skills. However, drawing and colouring-in was seen as a fun activity and I strongly believe that it enabled Anna to become the artist who loved to paint and enhance her creativity using the right side of her brain, which was not affected by her condition.

The stimulation and encouragement of each of these areas of independence, communication, creativity, and personal hygiene gave Anna a very good understanding of her own needs and abilities. It gave her the confidence to keep extending herself and to continue experimenting with other aspects of her life, such as enjoying fashion and fashion accessories, which she loved throughout her whole life.

She was able to draw a circle for her name when she opened her first bank account. Each time she walked into her bank, she confidently grabbed a handful of deposit slips and placed her signature (lots of circles) on every form. I realised she enjoyed signing those forms, so I encouraged her to focus on just one, otherwise the bank manager might have something to say about it. Mind you, I also thought they were so neatly and temptingly displayed that it was amazing they also seemed so perfectly kept—that is, until Anna entered the bank!

Lesson 19: Encourage independence, communication, and confidence

During these years, Anna's sister Claire was also instrumental in supporting Anna with her independence and communication, still using the Makaton sign language at home as well as encouraging her to use the toilet and embracing her differences. Claire would enjoy drawing with Anna, helping her up onto her rocking horse 'Star', and letting her go from one play activity to another. Anna's behaviour, although sometimes still aggressive, only escalated when she was not able to get her point across. This frustration, through the signing and increased communication, became less and less.

The connection between Claire and Anna was special. They had a bond where Claire would always look out for her little sister and protect her if ever she saw someone wasn't treating her right, which sometimes happened at the playground. Kids would often stare at Anna, wondering why she was so young developmentally but so big physically. Adults often did, too. It was at those times that you wanted to shout to the world that we are all different but the same! Many people who gave those stares did not have someone in their family or circle of friends with a disability and didn't understand. So we had to be tolerant and Claire certainly was. She always stood up for her sister and did it respectfully. I am very grateful, to this day, that Anna had such a wonderful sister and strong advocate.

Lesson 20: Acknowledge and encourage siblings to be supportive of one another

By this time I was working part-time so I was very grateful for my neighbours' support. On days when I was not back from work, Anna's school bus would drop her off at their home in the afternoon. Anna loved that, too. She really enjoyed being with their family where she played with their three children. Lyn and Trevor always treated Anna exactly the same as their other children.

This meant that Anna had another familiar experience, other than that of her own family with one sister. She got to see how it felt having other children around her, and when I went to pick her up she was always busy hanging out with them.

It became part of Anna's routine and she loved it. For many years we had this arrangement and it enabled Anna to blossom—her independence and confidence kept growing. Being consistently supported in her home, her neighbours' home, and at school gave stability and routine to her life. As she had autistic tendencies, this routine was essential for her wellbeing and personal growth.

Lesson 21: Provide routine and consistency

To watch the young girl who at pre-school age had been on the floor hitting her head and in a trance-like state, go from that 'inner world' to a world where she was connecting with, comprehending, and embracing life was truly mind-blowing. Sometimes Anna would return to that 'inner world' particularly when she was tired. When we saw her on the floor we simply asked her to get up and took her to the trampoline to stimulate her and she left her inner world behind. It's important in this story to include that phase of her autism.

I often wonder, if we hadn't thought it possible that she would come out of that 'inner world', what would have happened. Would she have reached her full potential? What would her life have been like? It really was, I believe, critical to her development and her quality of life.

In my view, to overcome the autistic tendency of living in an 'inner world' is life-changing. Having seen it with my own eyes being achieved through stimulation, through perseverance, through consistency, and through enabling Anna to feel valued in whatever she did, made a huge difference to her life—it was profound. She also had the drive, stamina, and fortitude to want to overcome the challenge and she rose to it. I believe Anna was remarkable in overcoming this hurdle and when she did her life continued to improve and we could see her true character shining through.

Lesson 22: Autistic tendencies can be reduced by stimulation and encouragement

When Anna left Mitchelton Special State School, it was evident that she had become more independent and her abilities had increased, and she had made many new friends. Her communication skills had certainly improved. She was able to string short sentences together. You would often hear her saying 'good girl' when she had achieved something like putting a jigsaw puzzle piece in its rightful place. Her frustration had disappeared altogether and she had become a bright, happy girl, who developmentally was at the age of a six-year-old. However, because of her confidence and her ability to connect with others, she was undeterred by this limitation as she did not see it at all. If anything, she just kept growing.

Soon she was a chatterbox, using her own lingo and signing with increased confidence. She often led the situation and became the 'bossy-boots' that we lovingly nick-named her. It was not uncommon for her to be heard saying, "Come here Claire!" and "What do we sing now?" and "Come on, Mum!" while she grabbed the car keys, ready to go out and do the shopping, having already prepared the list. She was ready to go. Fluffing around was Anna's pet-hate. If you were going to do something, do it now!

Lesson 23: Respect others' likes and dislikes

During this time, Anna's stepfather started to encourage her to swim. It was wonderful to watch. At first Anna was very reluctant to even get in the pool. In the end, Colin submerged his large frame beneath the water to entice her in. Then he showed her how to do the strokes so that she could see how easy it was. These antics went on for some months until one day Anna decided, like she did with the trampolining, that she was ready, and without any hesitation she made the leap into the water by swooshing her arms out and hoping that the rest of her body would follow and magically float in the water. After all, she had watched Colin do that many times—now she was feeling very confident and ready to take the plunge.

Fortunately he could see what was about to happen and once she had dived into the water he gently kept her afloat. It was a huge achievement for Anna. She was not only in the water but floating and, for the first time in her whole life at the age of ten, she felt the lightness of her body, the ease of movement, and the coolness of the water on her skin. She loved it.

Colin encouraged her constantly by saying, "Kick, Anna!" which over time she copied, saying it out loud to herself as she was swimming. It was quite amusing hearing her saying those words, followed inevitably by "Good girl!" Soon Colin did not need to say those magic words at all. By this time Anna, while telling herself how to swim, kept buoyant on her own. She had mastered it. Her record was twenty laps (without stopping), which was very impressive. It was as though once she started she was in the moment and it didn't matter how many laps she did, she was just enjoying herself.

Like trampolining, swimming was not only a fun activity but it was also strengthening her core muscles. It also improved her fluid retention as she had oedema which caused her to have swollen ankles and feet. When she swam regularly this disappeared.

Anna during her swimming jaunts met so many people who simply adored her and found her very focused once she got into the pool. She became more animated when she was in the water. She also became chattier, which often caused her to take an unexpected mouthful of water while she was swimming and busily giving herself prompts to kick. It was very entertaining for anyone who just happened to be in the pool at the time. Often they would remark on her sheer determination and stamina, particularly when they watched how many laps she did without taking a break. It was impressive and she certainly had everyone's attention and adoration.

Swimming was just so invigorating and stimulating for Anna. It played an important part in her life for many years and enabled her to keep fit and slim, improving her circulation.

My observations were that once Anna had experienced this exhilaration, it extended her in other ways too. She was more receptive to learning, she became stronger both physically and mentally, and she felt empowered and proud of her achievements. Most importantly, she found swimming just downright fun!

Lesson 24: Swimming enhances wellness, circulation, and fitness

Chapter 4
Community Building (UK)

At the age of twelve, Anna had become very confident and our family was excited about moving to the United Kingdom due to work opportunities.

For most families that is daunting enough having to move to the other side of the world, however when you have a child who has special needs it requires even more due diligence.

Once it had been confirmed that we were definitely heading abroad, I took a short trip to England to do my recce. I had to work out the logistics and demographics of where Colin would be working in London and where schools and universities were in the nearby counties as we wanted to live in the country.

Through the process of elimination I identified that a little village in West Sussex called Cuckfield best suited our family's needs. It was not far from Haywards Heath, which was on the Brighton to London line, making it a very easy commute. Brighton was just down the road so it was perfect for Claire as she could enrol in the University of Brighton and complete her studies.

The other appealing feature of Cuckfield, other than having a picture-postcard setting, was that it also had a special school, Court Meadow, with a very good reputation and a school principal who was well-known for her compassion and great leadership. I remember meeting her during my short visit and explaining Anna's history and, other than the school requiring Anna's full records to be sent to them in order for them to confirm her place, it felt like the school was 'just right' for Anna's needs. There was an ethos of compassion and care with innovation around independent living.

What I loved is that they focused on learning pathways including having an 'Independence Unit' attached to the school for the older pupils. It was like a high school with a difference. It really worked. There were so many enterprises and projects that they included in the program that really developed the pupils' desire to learn and become more independent. It was so refreshing.

Immediately I knew that Court Meadow Special School was going to work for Anna. It would build on her skills and increase her capacity for learning and development. It did all that, and more! Anna made so many friends at Court Meadow who became friends for life. The bond between those young people was special as they had an environment where they could be themselves and be proud of their achievements and their initiatives. I was also so impressed by the level of care that was taken by the teachers to acknowledge each pupil for the gifts they brought to the table and for their dedication and commitment.

Anna officially commenced at Court Meadow two months after my short visit to the UK. She never looked back. Those seven years at Court Meadow gave her wings to fly—as the school did with so many of the pupils who attended the school, some of whom have subsequently gone on to be UK celebrities known as *The Specials*. They have a very enthusiastic following on Facebook. Their public group has over 4,000 members.

Their Facebook page describes them:

> The Specials is an internet broadcast doco-soap about my sister and her friends who all have special needs and live together in Brighton. The documentary displays a 'fly on the wall' on how they live their life together and also on their own as teenagers with special needs and how they cope with everyday situations.

This is such a brilliant way to share their stories with the world. Go The Specials!

In my view, the more stories that are told bring us all closer together as a community. It enables more awareness and understanding to show that every person can contribute to society and be a valued citizen. We all have a story. We all have something to give back. We all want to be loved and respected.

Lesson 25: A stimulating environment increases learning and developmental potential

On my recce, I had thought that I would find a house to rent, but after looking at rental prices I could see that it was far too expensive. At that time the UK property market was down so I realised that if we were to live there for several years then it would be wiser to buy a property. During my short visit I identified the village that would meet our family's needs, selected Anna's school, and identified the university for Claire, as well as signed a contract to purchase a very quaint cottage in Church Street that overlooked the church yard and the beautiful 17th century church.

The house literally came to me. I remember touching the outside of the wall of the cottage as I walked past it to go under the lychgate into the church yard. It was such a beautiful place. I recall wishing that it was for sale. Knowing my time to look for houses in the area was very limited, I decided to go for a drive and just look around.

I remember stopping in at a real estate agency in East Sussex. They explained that as they were in a different county it would mean that we would need to look for another school for my daughter as Court Meadow was in West Sussex and each of the counties had their own schools and boundaries. It floored me. The lady saw my bitter disappointment. She offered to make me a cup of tea. We had a giggle about my lack of local knowledge and then she told me a story that her daughter was selling her cottage shortly. I asked where it was located and she said, "Cuckfield." I asked her, "Which house?" and then, to my absolute surprise, she explained it was the very same one that I wished had been for sale when I had been visiting the village earlier that day. Little did I know then that I would be returning later that afternoon to be shown around the inside of the cottage as a prospective buyer. When I was in the study overlooking the church yard I cried. I knew it was the right house. I always did.

There were so many wonderful stories to tell about Cuckfield, as it truly was so special. One I will share with you, in case you go there sometime and wish to visit the church—look at the baptismal font. You will see a crack in it. I was told that the font was cracked as Sir Oliver Cromwell's horse had reared up and had caused the damage. It struck me as strange that a horse would be inside the church but I got it straight from the locals' mouths and I also read about it in a book about villages on the A272 highway—so it must be true!

Regardless of the crack in the baptismal font in the church, Cuckfield was extremely appealing. It was like a magnet had drawn me straight to the village, the house, the school, and then I became fully immersed in the community. It was intoxicating.

I must admit that when living in such a beautiful part of England I often had to pinch myself that it was real as it was truly like the settings you see in *Agatha Christie*, *Poirot*, or *Midsomer Murders* (but without the murders).

We settled into our cottage and during the first week, an unexpected knock came at the door. It was the local social worker, confirming that Anna had been registered as having a disability and that the council was wishing to inform us of what the County of West Sussex could offer her in the way of supports, provisions, and services. It was most impressive.

I invited the social worker in. Although the furnishings were sparse, as our furniture was not due to arrive from Australia for three months, we found somewhere to sit while she opened up her folder, which contained pamphlets and a checklist. She explained that until we had lived there for three months (which was synchronised with our furniture arriving) we would have only limited support from the West Sussex County Council. However, she offered to go through what Anna would be entitled to once we had been there after that waiting period. It included a range of things including a link family option for which, she suggested, we should start the process as soon as possible as it usually took a few months to process if we were interested. So I asked her more about it.

The link family is a person or a couple who volunteer to offer 1:1 support to a child with a disability. It requires matching the link family with the child and this is done through a fairly rigorous process. The social worker further explained that, if I was interested in applying, it would mean that I list all of Anna's needs and the type of support that she would require. Interviews would take place with the prospective link family to make sure that it worked reciprocally.

We were very fortunate that, within six months, we had chosen our link family. When Anna met Sally they immediately clicked and the rest fell into place. Sally is now part of our family! That's how strong the bond is between us.

It made a huge difference as we had no friends or family in that area when we first arrived. It meant that I could join Colin in London for official engagements when Sally was able to have Anna overnight for respite.

It enabled Anna to socialise with someone other than her family and through Sally, Anna was able to widen her circles of friends. She loved being part of the group known as Kangaroos, which I recall we laughed about. Having an Aussie name seemed quite extraordinary and yet somehow it seemed so appropriate. Sally was a volunteer at Kangaroos so Anna was fortunate to have her there, where she could hang out and enjoy the program as well as be supported.

Anna, at this time, also became very involved with a group called Shine. It was a beautifully integrated theatre group offering sessions in singing, dance, and drama to youngsters aged up to nineteen, with and without special needs. Each member of the group who had a disability would be 'buddied up' with a mainstream partner. That partner took them under their wing, made sure they were always where they needed to be, and guided them in the art of staying focused on their performance—but always with a sense of fun and enjoyment. Anna joined in with the choir, where the teenagers were just so welcoming and keen to work alongside anyone from Kangaroos who might like to join them to learn certain songs for special integrated events.

One such event was our wedding in 2002, when several members of Shine volunteered to work alongside Anna so that she could sing with them at our celebration, in a performance that incorporated Makaton sign language.

It took six weeks of rehearsal to prepare for the big day. Every Sunday the girls would rehearse for a couple of hours followed by a pizza for lunch—it was so much fun. Anna was becoming very familiar with the songs, which included 'Something Inside So Strong'. She sang with great gusto, often beating the choir to the chorus as she just wanted to belt it out—and nothing was going to stop her! It was phenomenal to see her willpower as she was determined to sing those words and only use the Makaton when it was needed. She often looked like she was teaching the girls how to sing by the way she extenuated her mouth, as though she was giving them elocution lessons.

Lesson 26: Singing promotes creativity and ignites passion and joy

Living in Cuckfield was so special. It was a wonderful community. It had a heart. We experienced that every day when we lived there, as people passed by our front door that faced the pavement that led you under the lychgate through the church yard and to the woods. Many village locals would walk their dogs and naturally pass by our cottage. What was so uplifting was that many would stop and ask if Anna would like to join them for a walk and, most times, she would go along. It was just lovely having those moments where you didn't ask but it was offered. That was what made it so special, and yet for most people in the village that would have been seen as simply a neighbourly act.

The pre-school children who attended the community centre directly across the road from us would come out each morning for their walk, where they held a rope so that none of the children would wander off. The height of our front window meant they were able to see in, so I decided, not long after we'd arrived, to make it a display window where I would have themes such as teddy bears or Easter eggs. For the 50th Jubilee I put all the memorabilia on display that I could muster of the Royal Family. For that event it certainly was community at its best. The village was jubilant with the High Street being closed and tables from one end to the other filled to capacity with all of us joining in for lunch to celebrate the Queen's milestone. Of course, events like ours were replicated throughout the country that day, making it even more poignant to think that we were just one of thousands of groups celebrating in the same way. We were so blessed to be part of that celebration and to be part of our village community. We were so very proud.

Lesson 27: Embracing your local community enhances your quality of life

There was also the local pub, The White Harte, which was, as you would expect, nestled just across from the church. It was a stone's throw from our house. We found that particularly when we were transitioning to the new lifestyle it was an easy way to meet the locals and by frequenting it at a regular time during the week you would reunite with the same neighbours, who then became good friends. There would also be the unexpected visitors who would turn up, which would always add another dimension to the evening. It really was such a simple and yet special formula. Although I'm not a drinker, I went for the camaraderie and it gave another dimension to the day, particularly if you had been working, as I was at that time, at the Prince's Trust on a part-time basis while Colin had a much more high-powered position as Director of the Commonwealth Foundation.

Claire, who was living in Brighton so she could be close to her university, would join us regularly on a Sunday for a hot roast lunch and then we'd pop over to the pub to catch up with the locals. Sunday afternoons at the pub was particularly popular. Sometimes you could hardly move for the number of people all crammed into the bar, where some were playing darts while others were sitting at the tables telling yarns or standing up and huddled near the open fireplace. The White Harte became part of our routine and was important as a 'meeting place' for a range of people from diplomats to cleaners. It didn't matter. We were all the same—but different.

Anna, who just knew that when she went to the pub with us she'd meet a lot of people and dogs (as it was very common for locals to bring their dogs into the pub, which was interesting at times), was happy with all of her routine. This included the school bus picking her up from the Clock Tower car park and happily waving me goodbye as though I had done my duty and was given permission to do whatever I wished with my day. Clearly she was very preoccupied with socialising from the moment she got on the bus in the morning right up until she was dropped off in the afternoon. For her it was one big party—hanging out with her friends and, of course, learning new skills and knowledge.

Our lives were enriched and stimulated by the wide circle of friends we now had. Even inviting our neighbours over for wine and cheese on our pavement when the European sun was shining down upon us (which was a celebration in itself), and putting out a few chairs and a small table adorned with one bottle of wine and several glasses and nibbles, would attract the passers-by.

They would often join us on those long summer days and enjoy a good chat. I remember fondly many a time that we had our own mini-pub happening some days and wondered if we might be in competition with The White Harte. Fortunately it was never mentioned and was only seen as a neighbourly thing to do—quite an unusual one, as only an Aussie family would sit out on the pavement soaking up the sun! I should mention that our cottage did not have a garden, only a small courtyard that was very pleasant but too small to have more than a few people in it.

Another very fond memory was of Helen our postmistress. She loved it when Anna and I would go into the post office to send mail to Australia. She spoke of her family's desire to live there and we would often talk about it, as she had one family member already living in Australia. The relationship grew and Anna became very fond of Helen and her family. They had a daughter who was much younger than Anna but who was very kind and accepting of Anna's differences. We came to an agreement that on days when I was working longer hours, Helen would collect Anna from the Clock Tower car park and bring her back to the post office as their house was at the back of it and her daughter would also be home after school.

So this was another time when a neighbour befriended Anna and it became a rather special arrangement as she benefited enormously from being with them after school and it was mutual. There was growth for both girls and it was lovely to see their bond and connection growing.

The family did move to Australia and it's on my to-do list to try and re-connect with them to see how they transitioned to living Down Under.

Our neighbours diagonally opposite from us were extremely kind and, when we had virtually no furniture, they came bearing gifts. The first things they gave us were toys and books for Anna that we could borrow until we were sorted. They also made us food, brought some temporary furniture over, and literally embraced us from day one. They became very good friends, too. Some years later they moved to Lewes and we missed them very much. Anna would also go to their house regularly and play with their children and as Jill loved cooking special dishes for functions (including our wedding), Anna was in her element.

Then, looking down to the church yard on the left-hand side, there were several cottages all in a row. They were beautiful and reminded me of Anne Hathaway's Cottage. They were so appealing. We became very good friends with one of the families who lived in one of these quaint cottages. They loved creating and developing their homely cottage garden into something quite magical. It had birdfeed containers scattered throughout the trees and shrubs to invite the beautiful birds and a lovely pond with magnificent red-gold fish that looked extremely content. A bungalow was nestled right at the back of the garden, as though enticing you to stay. It really was so special to sit in their garden and watch the birds, feed the huge fish, and smell the aroma from their rose and lavender bushes. It was just so therapeutic.

Anna, as you would imagine, loved it there too. They embraced her—always showing her photographs that they took of the birds or of their recent travels and always having all the time in the world to stop and chat, no matter what they were doing. They, and so many of the locals, really gave their hearts and souls to us.

We were certainly blessed with a number of other special neighbours who also became very good friends. They were generous of spirit and we would often be at their places for dinner or barbecues. They would come to our place, too—it was special. I recall one afternoon in spring, Anna was invited to pick some apples from a neighbour's tree. They still remember Anna's face when they picked her up and she stretched her arms out and grabbed an apple with all her force and smiled from ear to ear. She was so chuffed with herself. Those moments are so precious and to share them with others in the community who had not experienced someone with different needs was, in itself, rewarding. Those memories will be with them forever, too.

Lesson 28: Share precious moments with others to bring them on your journey

What happens when the world of disability meets the world of diplomacy? It's not a trick question but for our family it was a reality for seven years while living in England. We had to attend many functions to which dignitaries were invited and, of course, we were too. I recall one occasion at Marlborough House in London when we had arrived at a reception. The banquet room was filled with high commissioners and people from many cultures. It was a true gala event.

Anna would introduce herself with a robust handshake and say, "Anna." She was not backward in coming forward, no matter what rank the person held, for she was oblivious of that. She would greet them all the same way. It was fascinating to watch the different reactions.

Some were quite indignant as they were caught off guard, particularly when she greeted them unexpectedly without any warning or diplomatic skills at all. Others were very warm and receptive and keen to ask her questions, which would often result in her moving onto the 'next one' as she would call them and shaking their hand. It was wonderful to see her confidence and to see that she rose to the occasion when she did need to be gracious. She worked the room beautifully.

At Colin's valedictory dinner, over two hundred people filled the Royal Commonwealth Society's hall. It was a very special occasion tinged with sadness that he had come to the end of his term as director, and there was also a sense of new beginnings as we were heading back to Australia after seven years in the diplomatic world. It had been filled with so many special occasions, meeting amazing people like Graca Machel and, of course, the Queen when the Commonwealth Writers' Prize recipients would receive their awards.

We would see her at many receptions and we were invited to a Garden Party at Buckingham Palace that was rather grand. We also loved staying at Cumberland Lodge at Great Windsor Park where we were able to enjoy weekend retreats and conferences. Our time in England had many special memories for us all. So this occasion was to mark the end of those seven amazing years and to farewell Colin's colleagues, friends, and associates.

He started his speech with, "Your Excellencies, Ladies and Gentlemen," and then paused, as a good orator should. However, Anna saw this pause as an opportunity for Colin to know that she was listening so she answered very loudly, "Yes," which sent whispers and looks of indignation across the faces of the guests in the big hall.

Colin smiled. He knew that voice and he handled it beautifully. "Oh," he said, "and Anna." He shared with the audience that Anna was his step-daughter and that if she commented throughout his speech, he would respond to her. So with those new boundaries set, Colin proceeded. He went on to thank the staff of the foundation and, at every pause, Anna would reply, "Good." It made the speech more animated, shall we say, and by the end of it

I'm convinced that Anna thought Colin had written that speech especially for her—she was just so engrossed from beginning to end. That's how much she revered her step-father.

At the end of the speech there was loud applause, and as people left the Great Hall not only did they wish Colin all the best for his future life and congratulate him on his speech, but they also wanted to meet Anna who, by this time, had become a star and was embraced by the guests at the reception that followed. Both of them were in their element that night. That's when the diplomacy world and the disability world became one.

Lesson 29: Take risks—expect the unexpected and let the different worlds entwine

Just prior to leaving the UK, Claire, Anna, and I were able to become dual citizens. We knew that it would be an opportunity, prior to heading back to Australia and having been in England for seven years, to formally become British citizens.

The applications were filled in, submitted, and approved. The letter explained that we would need to go to Chichester for the Citizenship Ceremony and swear on the Bible the oath of allegiance to Queen and country.

However, there was a slight problem. Anna's vocabulary was limited and although I could see her putting her hand on the Bible and saying, "Anna, good girl," I felt that might not suffice. I phoned the office and explained that Anna was not able to say the oath of allegiance and asked what options they could offer so that she could become a British citizen. There were no options. Unless she could say the oath, she could not have dual nationality in the European Union.

Well, that gave me an opportunity to advocate for Anna. She had every right to be accepted as a dual citizen and not to be discriminated against. So I went into action. I asked to speak to the highest ranking person in the system and explained to them calmly what I had just been told, seeking to confirm whether, in fact, it was accurate. I was informed that it was. I explained that I would therefore be making a complaint to the Anti-Discrimination Board. On hearing me utter those magic words, the woman explained that she would follow the matter up and get back to me. Knowing that the citizenship ceremony was only a week away, she realised it was urgent.

Within a half an hour the phone rang. She was very apologetic and explained that they would make an exception in this case. She asked me more questions about Anna's communication level. She listened intently. After a few minutes she offered a solution. "If you ask your daughter to put her hand on the Bible, when you say your oath, this will cover both you and your daughter. You will then be presented by the Mayor of Chichester with your certificates." I was very pleased with this outcome. I thanked her for being so helpful and finding a solution.

Sitting in front of me on my desk as I type these words I have a small photograph of Anna and me proudly holding our certificates and the mayor radiating a huge smile, dressed in her red suit and her blue mayoral medallion with the English flag proudly hanging behind us. The photograph shows that at that precise moment Anna and I had become British citizens. We both looked exuberant.

Anna was smiling and holding her hand to her mouth in a gesture that she often did at that time to express her coyness. However, she was also happy and proud. Although she didn't understand the significance of the occasion, Anna understood that it was a special moment in our lives as she could see it was an important and a memorable occasion.

Lesson 30: Know your rights and never give up

What was so touching was that the celebrant who conducted the citizenship ceremony knew Anna and me, and when we were greeted by her it made the whole experience even more welcoming and special. So what had started off as very stressful, finished as a day of great joy, and the memory will remain with me forever.

Claire, who was also being sworn in, elected to do her citizenship ceremony in Brighton one month later.

The three of us were proud of having dual nationality. I'm so pleased that we persevered and remained calm, even when we thought that the odds were against us. What also remains with us forever is our pride in being dual citizens and that we were able to deal with the situation in a way that gave a great outcome. The photograph is a reminder that we achieved our goal by mindfully questioning the system so that we were able to receive our certificates that meant so much to us. It will always be a special memory of a very special day in Chichester.

Lesson 31: Calm advocacy and innovative solutions encourage the best outcome

One of the most memorable moments, just prior to leaving our beloved Cuckfield, was the Balls' Bash, where we invited all the locals to come dressed as Aussies to our farewell event. It was to thank everyone from the village for their amazing support over the seven years that we had been fortunate enough to live in their community. During this time we had become regulars of The White Harte and had also held several fundraising events for the Ball Foundation, which we had established in 2002 just prior to our wedding. Our ceremony had taken place in the Town Hall, followed by a reception that was held at the Community Centre. Over two hundred guests had attended.

On this particular occasion, the farewell bash was more informal—it was simply to have fun. No intent to fundraise, just a lovely afternoon and evening of being together.

It was a perfect day. Those dressed in board shorts and thongs looked perfectly normal to us Aussies, who were used to seeing people dressed like that in our heat. Approximately one hundred guests arrived in all sorts of gear, ranging from demure costumes through to the most revealing. It was certainly a first for Cuckfield, seeing so many people dressed as though they were at a beach in Queensland somewhere. The fun began with the snags being cooked along with the onions on the barbie and everyone getting into the swing of the party. The bar tab was organised and everyone was enjoying their drinks and the food.

After a few hours it was late afternoon so we all gravitated into The White Harte's lounge area where there were lots of seats and tables and people could just hang out. At the end of the evening, when the bar tab was the largest ever for one person in the village, we decided it was time to wind things up. However, just before we got the chance, one of the village elders got up, quietened everyone down, and gave a lovely speech thanking us for the contribution that we had made to the community and saying that they would miss us. Several other people followed suit. It was touching to hear their kind parting words.

Someone sang out, "Does anyone else want to say anything?" Anna put her hand up. She walked over to where the others had given their speeches. There was silence in the audience and there wasn't a dry eye in the house by the time she finished. She imitated the actions and the intonations of the other speakers. Anna used her own dialect in which you could occasionally recognise a word here and there, but it didn't matter. She was being authentic. She was communicating from the heart. Throughout the speech she would pause, like a good orator should. The audience would then prompt her with 'Yes!' as though we were in a music hall. I suppose, after all, we were in England and they were well-known for their audience participation, so it felt perfectly normal.

Anna was given the floor and they gave her their full and undivided attention, encouraging her throughout the speech. The heartfelt speech went on for over ten minutes, which for Anna, whose vocabulary was up to five-word sentences, was a phenomenal achievement. Nothing was stopping her now—she was in her full glory.

Lesson 32: Believe in others and they will rise to it

It truly showed her confidence and that she trusted those around her to support her. The other speakers had been supported, after all, with loud rounds of applause, and now it was her turn. She had a lot to say and she said it in her way. She was also genuinely grateful for the love she had received while living in the village. Her quality of life had improved significantly. She had a circle of friends who were caring and supportive and she had a link family who gave tirelessly to her and who became part of her family. She embraced all her local communities—her friends from school, Shine, and Kangaroos. They were all woven like a tapestry through her life. She was happy.

At the end of her heartfelt speech, she uttered 'done', at which point everyone in the pub recognised that her speech was finished and gave her a standing ovation. It was so moving.

She was not one for wasting any time and walked purposefully over to me and grabbed my hand. "Come on Mum," she said, as though she had done her job well and she was ready to go home. We left everyone teary-eyed.

As we walked through the church yard in the light of the moon, I stared at Anna and what I saw was a determined, proud young woman who, at the age of nineteen, had just given her first speech. The moon's rays shone on her and she was radiant—a radiance that glowed from sheer joy.

"Anna," I said, "I am so proud of you. Your speech was just wonderful. You said everything that needed to be said. It was simply breathtaking." I kept staring at her as words weren't enough to express how I felt. My pride was welling up in me as I realised that Anna had just shown the world her pure authenticity.

She smiled back as though she knew too that she had just given the performance of a lifetime, a performance that had come unexpectedly out of the blue and without provocation and straight from her heart. It was intoxicating. She had touched everyone present and they, too, would never be the same. Our farewell event was indeed a success, and not in the way that we had anticipated. It was far more than a farewell—it was a legacy.

Lesson 33: Communicating from the heart is authentic

Chapter 5
Community Building (Italy)

In 1994 we bought a run-down farmhouse in Le Marche, Italy. In fact it was one-third of a house. It was so large that the owners, who had a long history of being custodians of the *casa* for many generations, wanted to sell just a small portion, which would enable them to restore their section.

The house, or *casa* as it is called in Italy, was the original *casa* in the district. It dated back to the 16th century. Nearby is an ancient monastery and a Roman bridge where the Metauro River runs through the village of Mercatello sul Metauro.

Mercatello is off the beaten track and in a valley surrounded by the Apennines. It is a rural community of farmers and locals who have kept the local traditions of their ancestors and who, for generations, lived off the land and are happy with their rich lifestyle. By rich I mean that they have a true sense of belonging and unity. They form a generous and humble community. I believe that this comes from the culture of embracing tradition and the family unit. Each person, from the youngest to the eldest, is treated the same. They are nurtured and loved. The elderly are seen and fully respected for their wealth of knowledge and pass on that knowledge seamlessly as they are part of the fibre of their community. People with disabilities are, like children, treated with great respect and dignity. It's as though they are revered for their purity and given their rightful place in the community. Unless you've experienced this first-hand, it is very hard to explain just how beautiful it is and how incredibly humbling it feels.

We were blessed to have been embraced by the community from the day we first came to the village. The renovation took many years but it meant that the *casa*—both our portion and the remainder of it—was in its full glory again.

Having a local *geometra* restore the *casa* beautifully ensured that the integrity of the building remained true to its past. He was a genuine craftsman, an artisan. Every detail was considered with great care. Understanding the importance of honouring the authenticity of the renovation was also important to the Mercatellese. They watched closely as the beauty returned to the *casa* and they could see it was being done meticulously. The last part of the renovation was placing the hand-made iron balustrading on the front porch. Just appreciating it and admiring every detail of its hand-crafted cast iron railings before they raised it up to its rightful place, was humbling. To mark the occasion, we had lots of onlookers share in the special moment when the *casa* was completed. It was wonderful to hear the murmurs in the crowd by the men who, if a piece of railing slipped a little as it was being raised into position, would share their concerns with each other as though it was a delicate piece of glass at risk of shattering. It certainly was precious, there was no doubt about that. Over several hours the deed was done. As Italians do so graciously, upon the last piece being in place, they clapped. Celebrations followed, with glasses of vino and lots of laughter. It was a very special moment, not only for us but also for the locals. The *casa* was important to them too. It had history and we were just its custodians.

We were fortunate to spend many a European summer at the *casa*, particularly when we were living in the UK. It is so easy to travel from England to Italy and we would either fly to Bologna or Rome and hire a car and drive to Mercatello sul Metauro, or cross the English Channel by the Channel Tunnel. It was fun driving the car into a carriage where the cars were butted up close to one another, motors turned off, where for approximately thirty minutes you were literally held captive until you came out the other side and arrived in Calais, France.

It was always a weird sensation when, toward the end of the journey, the train would start heading up towards land and you could feel the ascent and, at first, you couldn't see anything. Then as if by magic you could see, through the windows, the crops in the fields and the familiar sky. That was the moment when you knew that you had almost arrived at your destination. It was such a surreal feeling but it was exhilarating once you drove your car onto the road and were on your way again.

Lesson 34: Enjoy the journey, not just the destination

We did this trip quite often and I never tired of it. It was as though each time was the first time. It was so exciting, knowing you were crossing the English Channel without getting wet, and suddenly you were in a different country. You wouldn't know each time either what the weather would be like on the other side. It added to the intrigue.

One time we drove in January (in the dead of winter) through France, Switzerland, and then into Italy. We experienced a range of temperatures. The drive through the Swiss Alps was breathtaking with skiers jumping over the tunnel overhead and landing on the other side. We were mesmerised by their skilful jumps and agility. It was a wonderful sight to see, particularly as you drove through the cavernous tunnels not expecting the skiers to be using the slopes and the man-made tunnels as their playground. They appeared totally oblivious to us driving beneath them. Anna certainly got into the swing of it, saying her favourite word 'wow!' each time another skier miraculously appeared out of thin air. It made the trip go very quickly as we lost count of how many tunnels we drove through to then cross the border into Italy.

Later that day we stopped in Forte dei Marni, where they cut the beautiful marble from the mountainside. In stark contrast to France and Switzerland the weather here was bright and sunny. It was so unexpectedly summery that we enjoyed gelatos while walking along the promenade, where we came across many wealthy and colourful locals out enjoying the sunshine. As we walked along I saw something shimmering in the sun. It was on the pavement. I picked it up. It was a small obsidian elephant with beautiful stones adorning it. There was no one about and we decided that it would come home with us to Mercatello to sit on our mantelpiece. With our new-found elephant, we set off on the last jaunt of our journey, expecting to arrive in our village on the Metauro River by early evening. With this weather there would certainly be no hold-ups, we thought ... little did we know what lay ahead.

As we continued over the Bocca Trabbaria, winding our way up the Apennines like we were racing drivers in the Grand Prix, it felt exhilarating. Then snow started to fall heavily and the temperature continued to drop.

Soon it became clear that the area was in the grip of a fierce and heavy snow storm. We didn't have snow chains to put on our tyres so we drove very gingerly—no longer were we in Grand Prix mode.

As we got closer to Mercatello the snow ploughs were out on the roads. The depth of the snow was unprecedented. We continued through the village at a snail's pace. The village was hardly recognisable as it was covered by so much white and fresh snow on the ground, measuring, in some parts, a metre deep.

We drove into our street and much to our astonishment we couldn't see the driveway. It had disappeared under the voluminous snow!

Colin left the engine on so that we could keep warm as he braved the elements. He took his first step in the snow in his walking shoes, which were certainly not suitable for these conditions, and, even with his height of over six feet found himself sinking down until he was up to his knees in snow. No wonder we couldn't see the driveway!

He made his way carefully to the front door of our *casa*, unlocked it, and was inside for some time. I presumed he was igniting the central heating, which had recently been installed and which we had never used. It was the first thing we both commented on as we arrived, that it was a blessing that it had been completed recently.

In fact, Colin was not cranking up the central heating at all, as he could not read the instructions that were all in Italian. Instead he had lit the fire with the firewood that had fortunately remained dry and snug in the *casa*. He was concerned that with the temperature being well below zero, and without the fire being lit or the central heating on, it would be too cold for us. He decided that a little time spent establishing the fire would mean that we could snuggle up in front of it to get warm while we slowly unpacked the car and that we could, hopefully, turn on the central heating once he had worked out what the instructions said. It was a good plan.

As we had arrived three hours later than scheduled due to the conditions, it was dark and so we made sure Anna stayed safely in front of the fire while we unpacked the car, including our new acquisition—our obsidian elephant—which we placed proudly on the mantelpiece.

Once we had done that, it was time to focus on the central heating. I recall I had a torch—even though the lights were on it helped with reading the very small print that appeared on the inside of the unit. Colin had his Italian phrasebook, which meant that as soon as he got to a word that he didn't understand he would check it against the word in his little book, which clarified the instructions. However this took time; in fact, quite a long time.

Anna was happy in front of the fire but, unbeknown to us, she had decided that the fire needed stoking as she had watched Colin adding logs, sticks, and paper to it since we had arrived to make it keep burning. When we came out of the bathroom where the central heating unit was located we noticed that all the paper and twigs in the basket were gone, along with the knick-knacks from the mantelpiece. The fire was alight with orange and blue coloured flames that glistened in the light. It was well-stoked. Anna had taken over the role when she realised that we were busy and, miraculously, had done it safely.

Lesson 35: We are role models and our actions are observed by others

It wasn't until the next day that I saw in the bottom of the fireplace, in the cinders, something shimmering. I picked up the fire tongs and sifted it out from the ashes. It was the remains of our precious obsidian elephant.

The following day we were invited to have dinner at Ca Luce, which means 'House of Light'. Our friends had prepared a wonderful three-course meal for us. We were greeted by Francesca who took our coats and made a fuss over Anna, as Italians did all the time. We told her the story of our arrival and the demise of our elephant. She was very animated when she asked, "What did the elephant look like?" We explained it was only the size of a business card but made beautifully from black obsidian stone with the gems around the regal headdress on the top of the elephant's head as though ready to be presented to the Raj of India.

Francesca knew exactly what it looked like and there, before our eyes, she presented another—an identical one—which she had acquired many years ago. She explained that it was a good luck charm and that we must have hers as it was important to keep the omen that had come our way. We were so touched. We still have the gift she gave us that day in a very safe place. It was given to us with love and concern that we would continue to have good luck. That charm has stood us in good stead ever since.

Lesson 36: Sometimes gifts come in the most unexpected ways—treasure them

The precious memories we have of our time in Mercatello with Anna are endless. The kindnesses the Mercatellese bestowed on Anna were too many to mention. They simply adored her. From the moment they first met her, she was treated like a princess.

If we were in the village shopping, Anna would be given treats. Many treats. The baker would give her a tray of his freshly baked pastries. Our neighbours would knock at our door with home-made tortes that were absolutely delicious and intended not only for Anna but for our whole family. Many a time after being given fresh fruit and vegetables from their gardens, or a home-made torte, we would invite them to stay and sit under our fig tree which, depending on the season, provided shade and occasionally an unexpected surprise when a large, ripe fig plopped into a wine glass and often, due to its size, caused the wine to spill onto the red-checked tablecloth, giving everyone a fright. It made for good conversation, even when our Italian was not always fluent (particularly mine), and was very entertaining, unless, of course, the fig hit someone on the head! Amazingly it was still amusing to all concerned even when that happened! Other than when the figs were falling, the tree provided a sanctuary in our garden, where many a neighbour and visitor enjoyed relaxing and hanging out.

The daily event was also to take Anna to the village for her to have a gelato. She was spoilt as she had learned the art of watching the Italians when they spoke, using their arms and talking with great emotion. Anna would use this to her advantage beautifully. As soon as she stood in front of the open window, where the choice of gelatos was enormous, she would become more expressive and wave her arms around while pointing at several of the flavours and using the magic word that she had recently acquired; "Prego!" It did the trick. Not only did she get one scoop of each one, she would be given two scoops and sometimes many additional flavours would be added secretly. The cup would be overflowing and it was often a challenge getting it to the table in the bar, where we would cover her lap and the whole table with serviettes to ensure that half of it wasn't left behind. No-one cared. They just wanted to see Anna's happy face and her serious intent on devouring the gelato, focusing on nothing else. It was impressive—both the speed with which she consumed it and the amount she ate!

I honestly don't know how she didn't get brain-freeze from the large spoonfuls that she had in her mouth each time. Clearly it didn't worry her. The locals loved watching Anna gleefully have her gelatos and then, like any good Italian, become very animated and expressive all the way home.

Lesson 37: Enjoy the simple things and small pleasures of life

The *Palio* Festival is held annually in Mercatello. It has been running for over fifteen years. It is a satire of the *Palio* that is held in Siena. Instead of horses, they have donkeys, which as you can imagine makes for a very different race! There are four donkeys representing each of the parts of our community: La Colombara, La Pieve, San Martino, and La Baroccia. Each has different colours and symbols to represent their region and these appear on flags, t-shirts, umbrellas, caps, and all kinds of memorabilia.

La Colombara, which is our district, has a royal blue background with two white doves nestled on top of a chimney stack. It's so meaningful. My interpretation is that it means peace in the home—a sacred place.

The *Palio* is usually held in the second or third week of July. It runs for approximately seven days, culminating in the *Palio* donkey race around the *piazza* which, like Siena, has the sand put down on the cobblestones prior to the big day. The donkeys and of course their riders too are required to do several laps of the *piazza* in a race where you can never be sure if the donkeys are even going to move, let alone run. The donkeys don't always come around the lap with their rider on them either. It's totally unpredictable and always colourful, exciting, and fun.

Everyone sits expectantly in the stands that are erected around the perimeter of the *piazza* so that they have a bird's-eye view of the event. It's very popular with all ages and visitors come from afar to watch the race.

During the week a whole range of community events happen, including women's volleyball matches, men's football games, pasta-making in the *piazza* (which is then available at the food stalls), and children's games in the *piazza*. The race that is the most notable is the *biruncini* (pedal cars). For weeks prior to the *biruncini* race the teams—aged from young teenagers through to grandparents—practise going around the streets of

Mercatello, frequently passing our *casa,* which is very close to the *piazza,* to improve their speed and to master the pedal action on their wooden cars. It is taken very seriously. Everyone who is involved in the relay race has a responsibility to do the best they can for their team and to be as prepared and fit as they can be on the big day of the race, which is usually held the day before the *Palio.*

When the time comes for the *biruncini* race, the sound system is set up to make it sound like Formula One cars and each has their own pit stop where their wooden wheels will be changed at the end of each relay. It not only depends on the drivers but also the maintenance crew, who are poised and practised to change the wheels as soon as the pedal car comes into the pit stop, just like a real car race. There are four drivers in each race and they are required to do several laps around the *piazza.* Each represents one of the regions and covers the full spectrum of ages. The atmosphere is euphoric. The crowd is expectant after seeing so many of the competitors practising in the streets of Mercatello for many hours. They are keen to see the best team win on the day. It's anyone's race, as even with the strength and stamina of the drivers their crews have to be skilful and alert. One slight mistake could make the difference between winning and losing.

We loved watching the build-up to the race. It was enthralling and captivating as it had depth and purpose. It wasn't just a race. It was community at its best—everyone had a role to play, everyone was valued, everyone in the village participated in some way. Everyone took it seriously and everyone was motivated. It was a humbling display of community participation and engagement at its best.

The same could be said of the procession which is held the weekend of the *Palio*. There is always a theme. In 2002 it was the medieval period and everyone was dressed beautifully in decorated costumes, among them knights in shining armour and women with long, flowing, brocaded dresses with headdresses that matched the velours and fabrics of their robes. They were stunning. However, the day of the procession that year was hot. It was thirty-eight degrees in the shade. The participants were not in the shade; they were right outside in the street in front of our *casa* in the searing sun. That was their assembly point. We had the perfect vantage point, seeing them congregate and join the line, one by one, in their heavily brocaded costumes. The knights, with their full armour including shields and swords, were heavily adorned and rode magnificently on their stallions.

Within three-quarters of an hour, everyone was in their rightful places and representing their designated districts, displaying their banners that proudly represented La Colombara, La Baroccia, San Martino, and La Pieve. With the temperature soaring, they were all starting to wilt in the heat and in their heavy robes. We took out jugs of water and tried to hydrate them. It helped a little but we realised we really needed lots of water if it was to make a difference. We did our best to give water to the most needy and the procession was soon on its way to displaying, with great fervour, its medieval regalia and true civic pride for everyone to see. By then it didn't matter how hot they were; they were in the moment and nothing else mattered.

Lesson 38: Take pride in your community—participate and be engaged

Not long before the procession took place and before I was aware of the medieval costumes for the festival, I recall fondly an incident that from my point of view was incredibly exciting and romantic. However, from my sister's point of view it was sheer hell. Cherryl and her husband Bruce were in Mercatello for our marriage celebration, which was to take place that week. It was an informal affair as we had officially been married in Cuckfield in June. However, as we had several communities scattered across the globe with which we had strong connections, including Italy, Asia, and Australia, over the following six months we had small celebrations like the one in Mercatello in July. It was also to raise funds for the Ball Foundation.

The incident I refer to occurred when I was resting upstairs in the matrimonial bedroom (as that is what they call it in Italy) when Colin knocked on the door saying that there was a knight in shining armour on a stallion at the front gate calling out 'Suzi!'. I laughingly replied, "I have my knight in shining armour," to which Colin replied, "Well, you have another one and he's outside." I quickly got up as I found this quite amusing. Much to my dismay, there was a knight in shining armour on a stallion at the front gate, beckoning me to him. It was like a fairy tale. I had to rub my eyes to believe what I was seeing. Cherryl heard all the commotion and had come down from the attic, curious as to what was going on, wondering if this was what happened in small villages in Italy.

I walked past the front gate to the knight (as one does) and took his strong arm as he literally, in one swoop, catapulted me onto the back of the stallion with him. It was at this point that my sister was concerned. She kept saying, "Susan hasn't been on a horse before." She was perfectly right. Then, as she saw I was not coming down off the stallion, she started to take a video of the scene.

I'm not sure if it was because she thought it was entertaining or that it might be evidence should something go terribly wrong, as Gilberto and I galloped off into the sunset. Well, it wasn't quite the sunset, but it certainly was galloping and I held on for grim life.

We galloped up the narrow cobble streets through the *piazza* and onto the dirt tracks leading to the countryside nearby. It was exhilarating.

Gilberto, as any true knight in shining armour does, returned me safely to my front gate and swung me down so that I could show my sister that I was in one piece and satisfied with my adventure. I found out later that it is a long-gone tradition that, prior to a marriage being consummated, the bride-to-be would be taken by horseback to where the knight would have his way with her and then return her to the groom. I'm so pleased

I didn't know that fable when my hair was blowing in the wind as I galloped with my knight in shining armour through the streets of Mercatello that day!

Lesson 39: Always believe in knights in shining armour

Over the years many families stayed at our casa. This was initially made possible through the Ball Foundation that was established to make a difference to the lives of people with disability. It was only a small charity we had started when one of the Commonwealth Fellows had come to London and experienced the joy of having an electric wheelchair. When he returned to Zimbabwe, he found it difficult to use his manual wheelchair after the independence he had experienced with the electric one. He tried to obtain funding and found it was impossible.

When we heard of his need it was, along with our forthcoming marriage, a catalyst that ignited our passion to start the foundation for small grants, where we could raise funds each year for a specific purpose.

Through the generosity of the Cuckfield community, the past Fellow got his electric wheelchair and it was unveiled at our wedding reception. I recall the fanfare fondly when Anna was asked to unveil it. It had a beautiful satin cloth draped over it with brightly-coloured helium balloons.

When the time came for the electric wheelchair to be unveiled, Anna was asked to do the honours. With great enthusiasm, as she could feel the excitement that was building, she pulled the cloth off and up flew the balloons into the air as the audience clapped, whistled, and shouted for joy. It was a beautiful moment.

He received his gift soon after and the Ball Foundation continued to do its charitable work where 100% of the donations went to specific causes such as supporting Shine and Kangaroos and setting up an eye clinic in Sierra Leone. Thank you to Jeremy and Lin, who were trustees on the board, who worked tirelessly with us to achieve those goals.

As we had renovated the *casa* in Mercatello and designed the ground floor, which had previously housed the cattle, so that it was fully accessible, this meant that anyone in a wheelchair could stay there. So, the trustees of the Ball Foundation agreed that families from Cuckfield with children with disabilities should be able to enjoy the experience of full immersion, living in our special Italian village too.

Over the years, more than ten families had respite there. All we asked was that they write in the pebble book (aptly named due to the pebble-printed cover) on the sideboard about what they had done, what they had enjoyed, where they went, and any other important things they wanted to share. The pebble book became very special to us. There were so many heartfelt messages. People drew maps of walks they had gone on. They included names of restaurants where they had shared special moments.

The first thing I did whenever we arrived in Mercatello was to always read the pebble book while having a cuppa.

It was delightful to read the stories that continued to grow and it confirmed that the experiences had by each family were unique and had touched them in some way. I know when I would meet the families who had been that they were truly grateful and their lives were enriched by their visit. It also touched the Mercatellese as they got to meet many families with children with disabilities who came for short respite stays to our *casa*. As you would expect, the families were embraced by the community. Their children were revered and given many precious memories that would be with them forever.

Lesson 40: Be generous of spirit—give gifts that touch people's lives

The magic of Mercatello touches many people's lives and still does. After our return to Australia in 2004 I felt it was important to share not only with our UK families, but also with Australian families, what it felt like living in an authentic Italian village.

The outcome was the creation of the Authentic Italian Experience Custom Tour which was a flexible ten-day package that included experiencing full immersion into the Italian culture and community through learning the language (to enable the participants to know important words and phrases during their visit) and appreciating art and architecture. It was custom-designed.

The first group, thanks to my dear friend and business partner, Barbara, came from the Lismore University of the Third Age (U3A) as her mother-in-law was enrolled at the university. It was so exciting sharing the information about the region of Le Marche and its surrounds. Soon the first group had signed up for their trip in June 2005.

As I write this, ten years on, the group now known as The Italian Sisters have developed close and life-long friendships. We celebrate birthdays, Christmas, special events, and just enjoy our bond that was created all those years ago in the Apennines when each day was a concoction of new-found joy, friendship, and full immersion in the Italian culture. They took the word 'customising' to another level. Every day was truly unique and usually totally ad-libbed. The itinerary became defunct and instead they created their own daily experience with great fervour and anticipation. It was simply wonderful. Everyone loved it and the memories are etched on all of us forever.

Little did I know then, the meaningful friendships that were forged with The Italian Sisters have enriched all our lives and brought us all so much joy.

Lesson 41: Be brave—deviate and develop new plans, then embrace them

Some years passed after The Italian Sisters tours before it was time to re-evaluate how, when living in Australia, we could continue to maintain the *casa* as we were not able to be there enough ourselves. We had started new lives where Anna's education, our jobs, and so on meant it was difficult to go away as much as we would like.

It was time, we felt, to look at ways that we could keep a portion of our *casa* as the original owners had when we first bought it. It was seamless how this happened.

I was at the Port of Brisbane one day, talking about a fundraising cycle ride for SMARTCare Lifestyle Solutions (a foundation we started in Australia) and thanking the executive for his generosity. I explained that I would see him again in a month so that we could make sure the plans for the fundraising event were on track. His response, I recall vividly, was, "I won't be here. I will be squashing grapes." With that I knew that he was off to Italy and asked what part. He responded, much to my dismay, the region of Le Marche. I explained I knew it well and mentioned our *casa*. He then went on to tell me his vision: that he and a few other people from Brisbane he knew had been looking for quite a while to jointly buy a *casa* in Italy and that this was the reason for his forthcoming trip.

Knowing that we were also looking at the option of selling, the conversation then became more in-depth and we agreed that he would pass the information onto his partner once I had sent through an email with photos and a video, produced by the commune, of the Four Seasons in Mercatello. It was stunning.

He replied quickly to my email. He and his partner had organised an opportunity for a presentation of the *casa* in his office that week. It was a huge success. They had found their *casa*, not by going to Italy but by meeting me in an office in Brisbane and through a group of people who were already keen to buy a *casa* in the region where ours was nestled. It ticked all the boxes. Within a year of that first meeting, thirteen families in Brisbane bought shares in the *casa* and we kept ours— making it a fourteen-month cycle.

It has worked brilliantly. Again, meshing the two cultures together and building on the roots of trust and friendship that had been forged in the village, the new custodians were embraced. They too have stories they share with their children of the way their visits to the *casa* have enriched their lives and touched their hearts. Of course, the stories in the pebble book have continued to grow, and with the English and Australian families who have stayed there over the years it has become a wonderful diary of rich experiences and part of our heritage.

Lesson 42: Connecting communities enriches lives

Chapter 6
Transitioning (Australia)

Returning to Australia after seven years in the UK was both tinged with sadness, leaving our beautiful family and friends in England, and excitement, knowing that it would be the start of a new chapter in our lives.

It was the right time to return. Anna was at an age that she was ready for her transition to the next phase of her life. Having completed school in Cuckfield, she was now about to explore training options and become even more independent. It was one of the major reasons why we decided to leave the UK at that time as it gave Anna stability at an important time in her life, when she was transitioning. She was nineteen years of age. For someone with Ring 22, she was already breaking the rules and living well past her expected life-span. Anna, and our family, paid no attention to the statistics or the prognosis. She lived her life to the full and enjoyed every minute of it. Anna had no concept of age, prognosis, or limitations. She was just Anna, leading a normal life.

It was lovely to return to our house in Ashgrove, where we had lived during Claire and Anna's primary school years. It felt very strange that Claire had not returned to Brisbane with us. She had decided to remain in England. Leaving her was one of the hardest things I've ever had to do, particularly when we parted and had to say our goodbyes at Heathrow to her and Jake, her beautiful son who was only three years old when we boarded the plane back to Australia. Claire had started a new life so we understood and supported her decision, silently hoping that one day she would return to Australia. However, none of us have the power to make decisions for our children. It is their life and their journey. Claire knew that she was loved and she still is. She has lived in Brighton for eighteen years now and has another beautiful child, Mia. My two beautiful grandchildren, like Claire and Anna, are precious to me.

Anna was on her own now. Her sister wasn't around to give her the nurturing and support she had received before. Now it was only on special visits that she would see Claire when she came back to Australia or when we went back to England.

Of course there was Skype, which Anna loved, as Claire was so animated and inquisitive, asking Anna lots of questions and calling her 'sweetie' and other endearing terms, which was lovely to hear.

For the most part, Anna would just be glued to the computer screen, watching her sister talking to her, where she could just sit and be totally absorbed in the conversation through simple gestures or the occasional utterance of 'good girl' or 'Claire!'. When she was ready to finish the conversation, it was 'Bye!'—even if Claire was in the middle of a sentence. If Anna felt it was time to end the Skype session, it wouldn't matter what was happening, she would simply get up and walk away from the computer. She would either try to find a DVD or give me the keys to the car to indicate that she'd like to go out, particularly if we'd talked earlier about shopping or an outing. She could be very determined and would not let any opportunities pass her by. Nor was there any debriefing or conversation after the Skype call at all. As far as Anna was concerned it was 'done' and she had moved on.

Lesson 43: Circumstances may change but it is the precious moments that count

It was fun reconnecting with the community and identifying options for Anna so that she could enjoy her new life.

What surprised us upon returning was that Anna could remember, seven years on, exactly the route home from the airport. As the bags were put in the taxi, Anna quickly got in and started telling the taxi driver the instructions. They were clear to us, but perhaps a bit vague for him when she would say 'left here' or 'straight on' and use the opposite sign for left and right.

Nonetheless she was focused and we found that she did this in every country where we lived. She would always know the directions, particularly as we got closer to the destination. It was fascinating that her memory retention for directions and her ability to navigate were so good. She certainly didn't get that from me! I was in awe of her navigational skills and her sheer excitement that she would get us home.

Lesson 44: Acknowledge and celebrate strengths and build on them

It was joyful looking at courses in which Anna could participate, including TAFE (Technical and Further Education) where she enrolled in a computer course so that she could communicate in other ways. She loved it. Her favourite was a duck game where, as she got the mouse on the correct spot, the duck quacked. She often giggled as it really tickled her fancy. It was also helpful that, while she attended the course, Anna had a volunteer, or aide, who supported her. It worked a treat.

Anna learnt a lot about using the mouse, how computers worked, and how to use the keyboard. (She loved pressing random letters on the keyboard so that there were multiple letters appearing across the screen as if by magic!) It was very empowering for her. For years she signed off my emails when I'd ask her to write something to Claire and she would confidently sit at the keyboard and press usually the letter 'M' for Mum, 'A' for Anna, and 'C', which covered both Claire and Colin, which was helpful. So she knew what the letters stood for and she continued to build on that knowledge.

I was surprised, not long ago, when Anna confidently pointed with her long finger at a menu and with great poetic licence dragged it across the page as though she was deep in concentration before selecting the item. She had pointed to the word 'omelette' and, indeed, she wanted an omelette. I asked her that day whether she could read the word in the menu. The sheer look of indignation was enough to tell me that it was the wrong question to ask. I clearly could see she could read it—after all she had gone to great pains to show me and how could I have been so blind not to see that? When it came to food, Anna could do anything, and as I found out that day this included reading the word 'omelette'.

Anna also became involved in a hospitality course that she loved. They made wonderful recipes and she would come home with vanilla slices, quiches, and various pastries. It was great as they had a big kitchen that enabled Anna's group to get a feel of what it would be like to be a chef and to give them support making their favourite dishes.

Of course, Anna had another mentor when it came to cooking: Colin, who loved to cook the evening meal. He often made large batches at a time to enable food to be split up into smaller-sized meals, which was a good way for our small family to have home-made frozen meals available at all times, particularly when the chef was away or not in the mood for cooking. Considering I would, when cooking for myself, keep it very simple with salads, fish, and chicken, this was one area that I certainly did not find stimulating so I always felt pleased when Colin and Anna were in the kitchen as they both gained so much from it. They had fun. Anna was engaged and Colin was at his happiest preparing food, as it is his way of showing his love and care.

Often I could hear Anna saying her favourite words so I knew that she was in full swing. I would see her stirring the stew in the saucepan as it heated over the stove. She loved that task as she could smell the aromas wafting into her nostrils as she stirred with all her might. It was great for her to be so involved from start to finish. Sometimes she was also known to help with getting the ingredients out of the fridge. This was often fraught with danger as the cheese, milk, eggs, and meat often got taken out of the fridge with great gusto, which resulted in the ingredients sometimes being worse for wear or even not making it. We learnt to ask her to focus on things that were robust so that the eggs, over time, were safe. That was one ingredient we tended not to mention after we had experienced several interesting and sticky incidents over the years.

I often laughed when Anna and I made pikelets together, which became our speciality. The pikelets often landed anywhere but on the tea towel that was on the tray neatly placed next to the stove. It was like being in a kitchen with a pizza-maker who throws the pastry around and makes it go up in the air to lighten the dough. Well, perhaps that's what Anna thought she was doing, as it did resemble that scene often! Whatever pikelets did make it to the tray were handled with care, as often it was a limited number from the batch of batter that we had whipped up. They were devoured with jam and cream shortly after the baking antics were completed. I recognised them, even at the time, as precious moments that are now poignant memories.

> *Lesson 45: Be mindful of precious moments that then become poignant memories*

Over the following years, Anna continued to love all her educational experiences. From the hospitality course she then diversified into a horticulture course, which she also loved. She was like a sponge. She was taking on new challenges like potting plants, weeding, and learning how to plant vegetables, even with her limited fine motor skills. She found other ways to do things. If she couldn't hold something in one hand, she would do it with two. Nothing was stopping her. If she saw a job and she wanted to do it, she would find a way. She was resourceful. That of course is the key to learning—to be adaptive and innovative and keep extending yourself to achieve the goal that may have seemed impossible at first.

That trait, which kept Anna in good stead, is a wonderful quality. Be prepared to change how you do something even if doing so will take you out of your comfort zone. It is a huge learning curve. Once acquired, it brings hope, joy, and meaning to what could otherwise become frustrations and limitations.

Anna never saw her limitations. She gave anything a go and it was really starting to show during this time in her life. Her swimming became stronger. The lap count was increasing all the time and was constantly revised whenever we were asked by family and friends how many laps Anna had done. She kept doing more and more and more. My recollection was that she got up to twenty laps without stopping.

> *Lesson 46: Be adaptive, responsive, and prepared to change how you do things*

Her ability to walk, at that time, was also impressive. Often we would head off from Ithaca Creek at the foot of our cul-de-sac in Ashgrove with our backpacks on. I'd have my mobile phone as I wouldn't know how long we would be gone. Anna's power-walking meant that we could easily be away for hours and nothing would stop the flow. Anna was purposeful and mindful. I was purposeful and mindful of Anna and aware of every step as there were times when I wondered how we would walk back! A few times I recall, after four-hour walks, that I would ring Colin and ask him to pick us up as the idea of walking another four hours back was daunting for me! I know that Anna would have been fine with it as she was so fit and healthy from all her outdoor hobbies, which included swimming, walking, and gardening. She was powering.

> *Lesson 47: Keep fit and healthy—enjoy the outdoor life whenever you can*

Her other passion was being an artist. She loved creating designs and using different techniques. She wasn't adept with a paint brush but she could use her fingers, and sometimes she had little stamps with symbols on them that she would press on the paper to make interesting creations. She had a very unique style in which you could start a painting with her that she would then draw her circles on and apply colour to with different media like chalk, charcoal, and acrylic—all of which gave Anna her own brand, her own signature. She adored her time at Access Arts where not only could she paint and be creative, but she was also supported and encouraged to extend her skills to different genres and different media. She loved experimenting and I have several large art envelopes filled with her work that she completed over many years. It may well be that as part of the celebration of Anna's life, I select from the pieces and put on an art exhibition in her honour where her art can be enjoyed again. Like the famous artisans of a long-gone era, she has left a legacy of her beautiful creations for the world to see.

Lesson 48: If you are an artist, leave a legacy of your beautiful creations

Anna loved to work with clay, too, and recently a dry clay figurine with eclectic hair sitting in a squatting position came home in bubble wrap on a cardboard base. The arms of the figurine were sitting next to it, along with lots of the clay strands of hair. Unfortunately his nose had come off, too. I loved repairing the figurine to its former glory and he really does look content. He came with a clay towel decorated with some intricate detail. I could see that Anna's intent was that he was sitting on a beach towel somewhere on a secluded beach. That's what I gleaned from the pottery pieces that had been returned with care that Anna had lovingly made. They needed to be repaired and restored to their full glory. The rejuvenated figurine now adorns my desk. As I write this story, the desk light shines on him sitting proudly in place on his hand-made clay beach towel with designs impregnated into the clay and with little tassels on the ends. I painted a scene of rolling surf and sand on a canvas, which sits in the background. He's now found his rightful place and looks very content and peaceful. He's come home and watches me like a wise owl, making sure that the words come through me onto the page as they have flowed ever since I started writing this book.

He knows, as I do, that Anna would want these lessons to be shared and like his full restoration, the pieces of Anna's life are now being put together like a jigsaw puzzle where each piece is slotting in where it is meant to be. It's strange—though I had this book inside of me all the time, it's only now, when I can draw from the learnings, that they all make sense and that I can see why it's so important to capture them. It is the powerful lessons that Anna so carefully crafted throughout her life that now give me the ability to share her wisdom and knowledge with you through this storytelling.

Lesson 49: Capture and share the important lessons of your life

Several years after our return to Australia, I felt it was time to move from our house in the western suburbs to relocate closer to the city—ideally overlooking the Brisbane River. I had an image of our place being in the hub, just like in Cuckfield and Mercatello, where we would be within walking distance of the main town and able to, just at a stone's throw, be in the thick of it. I loved the feeling of being central where you could easily connect with others and, also when you chose, to feel you had your own sanctuary. These were learnings that I took from our other homes across the globe and what, for me, had worked well.

I remember that I took a long time to find the right place. A friend of mine who is a real estate agent in Brisbane gave me good advice. He said, "If it doesn't ring your bells, don't buy it." I paid attention to my feelings and, as I had done in Cuckfield, knew when the right one touched my soul.

The right place actually came to us. We did not find it—it found us. It is another story that makes me smile when I recollect it. For it's another piece of the jigsaw puzzle that fits perfectly in its place. I can see it clearly now.

At the time, we had a wonderful boarder staying with us in Ashgrove. She was an opera singer and one of the Italian Sisters. Kate and her mum, Carole, had both come on the Authentic Italian Experience Tour and, at the time, were living in Lismore. However, Kate was offered a fantastic opportunity of working with Opera Queensland as she had a beautiful operatic voice. She was keen to take up the role. When we heard, it was a natural transition for her to live with us while she found her feet and permanent lodgings. For us it was just downright fun having Kate stay as she would practise her singing either down at the park below our house or, sometimes, in her bedroom. Either way, it was breathtaking to hear her voice and we knew she would go far with her singing career.

It was during this time that we met a young man who was volunteering as a valet at the Royal Brisbane and Women's Hospital. We connected with him on our first visit there when Anna had been unwell.

He was very courteous and explained that he was on work experience as part of his rehabilitation after having had a recent stroke. Through conversation with him, we found out that he lived in New Farm with his Italian mum and we continued to keep in touch.

Lesson 50: Trust that the right people are on your journey

One day he invited Kate, Anna, and me for a drive to New Farm and said that he would show us around as none of us had really been part of that community, which was rich with Italian culture and close to the city. It ticked all the boxes. With the invitation, I became the chauffeur and he gave us a guided tour of this beautiful suburb known as the peninsula due to the Brisbane River winding its way around it from each side. You can easily lose your sense of direction as the river confuses you because of its meandering shape. On the drive, we came across a unit for sale. It was in a location that I had never spotted, even in my search for a home in this vicinity. For some reason I had never gone down to this part of the suburb and it was beautiful. I wrote the details down on a bit of paper that I had with me and knew that I would be calling the real estate agent when I got home.

The unit was located right on the river, constructed in a Mediterranean style and comprised of thirteen units. It was four storeys and had appeal. It certainly had my interest and it had captured my heart.

After our tour, I set about phoning the agent, who informed me that there would be an open house on Easter Saturday the following weekend. I asked her a few questions to find out whether the unit was suitable as I had a checklist. It met that too. I was very excited.

During that time my dear friend Barbara's daughter, Philippa, had passed away from a brain tumour, and Carole and Kate had by this time become close friends with Barbara. After boarding with us, Kate relocated to live with Barbara who lived in Red Hill, Brisbane. They had so much in common with their passion for opera and dance. Carole would visit Kate regularly and became very close to Barbara, too.

So when the day of the open house arrived it was decided that we would all go together, just prior to lunch. We had been busy that morning helping Barbara around her house. When we arrived at our destination there were a lot of people in the unit. We could see from the street that the front porch overlooked the river and the cul-de-sac, which was a vantage point. You could watch the City Hopper and City Cat (the Brisbane City council river transport—the City Hopper is the older, slower boat and the City Cat is the catamaran) come to and from the Sydney Street ferry terminal, right ahead of you. If you turned around, you could see the visitors walking on the front deck of the unit. The tops of their heads were in view, too, if they were sitting at the large round table right in the corner in front of the hedge.

Barbara, Carole, and Kate decided to sit down by the river and let Colin, Anna, and me go and see the unit. It was so exciting. It rang my bells, that's for sure. It was accessible, had three bedrooms, views of the river, two bathrooms (one of which had been modified with a shower suitable for Anna with a hand rail), a side courtyard, and a huge front deck. As we walked out onto the deck there were people sitting at the outside table reading documents. They were focused and clearly very interested in the property. We were just enjoying the whole experience of seeing such an amazing place where you could literally watch the world go by and yet have everything at your fingertips.

Anna went into action. As each boat came into the ferry terminal she would call out loudly and with great appreciation 'nice boat' followed by 'wow!'. She also did this with great gusto. She loved it. Her intensity was so powerful that it even interrupted the prospective buyers, and unbeknown to us, sitting not far from Barbara, Carole, and Kate, was the owner. She was observing with great interest who was viewing her unit. She could see the fervour. She could hear Anna's voice wafting down to her, declaring her love for her unit. As we were leaving, the real estate agent asked if we were interested in the unit. I smiled and answered with great enthusiasm, "Definitely!" However, my concern was that it might be slightly out of our price range. She responded very unexpectedly. "If you are interested, the owner is keen for you to put in an offer." I gave her a ballpark figure. She nodded. We then agreed to meet up at a nearby café two hours later. What had just happened changed our lives forever.

Lesson 51: Value friendships and what they bring to your life

Anna had woven her magic. The owner had heard Anna's enthusiasm. She wanted her beloved unit to go to a family, not an investor. The other prospective buyers were investors.

We went back home with Carole, Barbara, and Kate and told them of our good fortune and that we were very excited and needed to do a few sums before our meeting. Carole had made soup before we'd left so we enjoyed that together and then Colin and I had time to discuss our situation before leaving to meet with the agent. Anna stayed with the women and was kept very busy as they all loved cooking and were busy preparing the meal for that evening.

The agent had her clipboard with the contract tucked safely inside it. We had coffee. We talked and agreed on a price and conditions and signed the contract. The deed was done. We trusted in what was going to happen over the next twenty-four hours. We hoped that our offer would be accepted.

When the phone call came through the next day I was down in Barbara's garden doing some weeding and Colin was out getting some hardware as he was doing some maintenance for her. "It's the agent!" Barbara sang out. She brought the phone down to me. I couldn't move. Then I realised how important it was and that the unit had touched my soul. The conversation, thank goodness, confirmed that the owner was indeed happy with the conditions and was going to sign the contract that day. I was euphoric.

It felt as though, thanks to Anna, our dream home had just been delivered to us with a big red ribbon wrapped around it. It had come to us not by chance but by serendipity. It was meant to be. It was an important time in our lives and we had much to celebrate. In fact, the final piece of this jigsaw was not completed until recently when I realised the higher purpose of our move here. Anna, I believe, already knew that from the day when she proudly confirmed the setting was 'wow!' that it would become integral to her quality of life, as did the 'nice boats'. Our beloved unit overlooking the Brisbane River that ebbs and flows has provided a sanctuary—a sacred place where we are blessed to have caring and loving neighbours who, like in Cuckfield and in Mercatello, have given us so much support and have embraced our family.

Lesson 52: Awaken your spirituality by trusting in synchronicity

Chapter 7
Medical Learnings

It was the week before Christmas, 2005. We were having a wonderful holiday with special friends from India – Rajesh, Martha, Sulheil and Tariqa – who were staying in the unit next door to us at Centrepoint in Caloundra. Rajesh had been our best man at our wedding in Cuckfield in 2002 and it was so lovely that we were able to reunite our families again for another special celebration.

We had a bird's-eye view of the Pumicestone Passage overlooking Bribie Island. It was such a breathtaking sight. Watching the world from Level 14, the top floor of the building, was just so exhilarating and from there you could see the skydivers coming down to land on Bulcock Beach directly below us.

They were gliding with such ease and beauty as though they weren't afraid at all of the heights, but instead were enjoying the beauty and the vista below them. They were experiencing freedom. We were experiencing wonderful entertainment.

Anna would say her favourite words of 'wow!' and 'good' as she watched them drop from the sky. I was watching how they were harnessed into their seats below their canopies. It fascinated me that they looked so comfortable and that we could see them so closely as to see exactly what they were wearing. I found myself mesmerised by them. They looked perfectly peaceful, hanging in the air and gliding in the breeze with not a care in the world.

Staying at Caloundra was always so much fun as we had been fortunate enough to purchase our unit prior to going to the UK, and upon our return we were able to use it for up to four weeks during the year. For the rest of the time it was rented to holidaymakers who loved it and would make prior bookings for a year in advance. We did too. We loved being there at Christmas so that we could enjoy the festive season at the beach and make the most of being back in a warm, sunny climate. We embraced it after seven years of English weather.

So it became a tradition that we would book it for that time of the year and enjoy the peak of the summer holidays. I would assist Anna, after her bath early in the morning, to get her togs on, go down to the pool, and enjoy the cool water on her skin and embrace her love of swimming. She would take a while to get in (like her mother) but after she had immersed herself in the pool she was away. Nothing could stop her.

Our friends were amused, when we went down to the pool, at Anna's swimming antics and how she came alive. They were so happy to be enjoying time with us in Caloundra. It was their first visit to the Sunshine Coast and they had planned their trip so that they could join us for a special family holiday during a very sacred time of year. We were all excited, knowing we would have precious time together. We didn't expect it to go quite the way it did.

Lesson 53: Embrace sacred time with your family and friends

Three days before Christmas Day, Anna was enthusiastically swimming. She had completed eighteen laps when she stopped. She simply stopped dead in her tracks. She didn't say her usual word 'done' and she seemed disorientated. Colin wrapped a towel around her to make sure she was warm as she had started to get goose-pimples, even though the air was warm and the temperature over thirty degrees. It was unusual.

Then we noticed Anna was unstable. We thought that she must have overdone it, so we got her upstairs and onto the bed. The very fact that she stayed on the bed was also strange. For Anna, lying down was something you only did at night-time. She made no attempt to get up. Then we noticed that her eyes were rolling and she was not coherent; then she became violently ill. We called the ambulance, which took us to the Caloundra Hospital.

After Anna went through to the emergency department, they did the usual blood tests and came back with no evidence to suggest that she had anything other than a virus and we were told to take her home to rest.

We returned to our unit, hopeful that their diagnosis was right. We felt things were far from right. They felt very wrong. Anna was different. She was not settling and was walking aimlessly around the unit as though she had lost her way. She was confused and her eyes did not look right. This went on for twenty-four hours, so Christmas Day was a bit of a blur. We decided to head back to Brisbane and take Anna to the Royal Brisbane and Women's Hospital. We did this twice, and both times they gave the same advice as the Caloundra Hospital; that her blood tests were clear and that she probably had a virus and should come home and rest. On the third visit there I didn't accept their prognosis. I was anxious. I was in advocacy mode, as they weren't listening. Anna didn't normally walk aimlessly around, nor was she usually quiet and disorientated. She had changed. In my view, she needed a CAT scan to see if there was a neurological condition causing her symptoms.

It may seem like a perfectly logical next step to anyone else. However, they saw Anna as a person with a disability. They presumed that her cognitive skills, including speech, were always limited. They couldn't see that she was different from her normal behaviour. I could. I caused such a commotion, as they were still not listening, that they called for a security guard.

Once he had come I could tell him my dilemma and ask for his assistance so that I could see a social worker as my daughter needed urgent medical attention, which she wasn't receiving. It worked. I settled down once I knew he had called for the social worker, who came to see Anna and me shortly after. She could see that Anna was extremely ill and required medical assistance. She listened intently.

At her request, the doctor and his team returned to our cubicle, where Anna was becoming very agitated. The social worker could see what was happening and was able to explain that I knew my daughter better than anyone else and that I was acting in my daughter's best interests. She explained that I wasn't 'a mother being hysterical' (which is how they had seen me), but a very concerned and worried mother. It was clear Anna's condition was worsening and that, since her turn two days ago, the hospital visits had not given any comfort to Anna or improved her situation at all.

Lesson 54: Don't accept the status quo—defend your loved one's rights

Suddenly Anna started having a fit and she became unconscious. Buzzers went off, people ran from all directions, and they worked together on Anna to resuscitate her. Finally she regained consciousness and they were now listening. They could see, like I had since Anna became ill, that she was in serious trouble. It was the first time in her life that she had shown signs of epilepsy. They sedated her so that she could have a CAT scan.

Immediately following the scan she was rushed into Intensive Care Unit (ICU). The scan revealed that a brain tumour, deep in the thalamus, had haemorrhaged. Anna was in the unit for several days as they kept a watchful eye on her condition while she became more stable. During this time a neurosurgeon was appointed, who explained to us that it was a miracle that Anna had survived. He hadn't known anyone who had.

It was clear that Anna's life would change from that point. It took us completely by surprise. One minute she was a healthy young woman swimming laps in the pool and now she was facing the fight of her life.

The neurosurgeon suggested that once Anna was stable and out of ICU, they would do an MRI with contrast to give more detail so that they could identify what type of tumour it was and what options there were to improve Anna's circumstances. After having the MRI, we were shown the scan. It was easy to see, even to the untrained eye, where the tumour had haemorrhaged, from the dark colour around the greyish mass.

After speaking to the neurosurgeon and his team, it was agreed that a biopsy should be undertaken to clarify whether it was benign. It would mean that Anna would have further medical intervention. We explained to her that it was necessary in order to give her the best outcome. She understood and gave her consent. She just wanted to get better and that's what we focused on.

We kept her as happy as possible during this very difficult and stressful time by filling her room with familiar things from home, amongst other things. Photographs on large cardboard sheets adorned the walls of her private room in the hospital so she could see family members' faces and feel safe. We brought her favourite books and clothes in, so that made her feel good too. We realised that she didn't understand what was happening to her, so giving her familiarity in the best way we could brought her some comfort.

> **Lesson 55: Provide a safe, familiar environment and nurture a sense of belonging**

For the first time in her life, Anna's cognitive development proved a challenge, as there was no provision in the Royal Brisbane and Women's Hospital for them to understand her needs unless I was by her side. Even taking her blood tests required treating her like a young child, using techniques that relaxed her as much as possible, such as singing, distracting her by reading her favourite book, or simply reassuring her that it would be over and done with quickly and that she would have a reward. Our strategy was that as soon as the test was done we would resume whatever we were doing, like watching a DVD, so that it caused her minimal trauma.

These person-centred techniques and approaches seemed, at that time, foreign to the nurses, as they were used to just coming in to their patients and taking blood tests without any fuss or bother.

If we had been in a paediatric hospital then Anna would have been treated differently; they would have taken into account that she may be frightened and scared of a nurse putting a needle in her arm and be offered an incentive like jelly beans or stickers. This certainly was not the case in the adult hospital.

I was surprised that they didn't have flexibility in cases where their patients had special needs and required the same level of support as a child to help them feel safe in an unfamiliar environment, particularly when they didn't understand why they were there and what had happened to them. Rather than see this as a negative, I found my role as Anna's advocate going into full swing. As the team would come in for tests, we would make it a game. They joined in. Once they felt comfortable, and could see the difference it made to Anna, they became more person-centred and empathetic. For the most part, as they returned on their next shifts they became more willing to approach Anna with less discipline and more heart.

They warmed to Anna and, as we were ensuring that they were on the journey with us, soon we saw them adopt very different approaches. They were being gently guided to meet Anna's needs, including giving her jelly beans and stickers to reward her for her co-operation.

They were acknowledging and appreciating her difference. To see them more mindful and aware was very uplifting and comforting.

Lesson 56: Mentor others in the art of being person-centred

Anna was in the hospital for several months. She became very well-known in the ward as during her stay she adopted an active routine in which, after the rounds of the doctors, she would have her shower then walk around the ward, outside in the courtyard, and on good days in the sunshine and under the trees with me. She was certainly not interested in staying in her room if she could avoid it.

She also loved having visitors and was blessed to have family visit; like my sister Cherryl who was there many times, particularly when Anna was most vulnerable and having chronic episodes of seizures. Cherryl became an expert in guesstimating the time between seizures and how long they would last. It was lovely to see her connection with Anna strengthen and I appreciated that she was there to support me, too. It made a huge difference. There were times when her daughter, Melynda, would come to the hospital with her beautiful children. Sometimes Mel would pack a picnic lunch and we'd go down under the trees and we'd all enjoy being together. It was lovely.

My wonderful work colleagues came regularly to visit. I would find them very involved in storytelling by creating their own amazing stories they had woven from words that sounded like they had been plucked from mid-air. In fact, they had been skilfully put together. If they were in the middle of the game I learnt to just join in, as they took it very seriously and so did Anna. There were certainly some very elaborate stories told on those special visits and Anna loved it. I was simply blown away by their generosity, kindness, and creativity. I could see why they worked in the sector—their hearts were in it.

Lesson 57: Invite others into your world to build awareness and empathy

The biopsy revealed that Anna had a benign, slow-growing pilocytic astrocytoma that she had apparently had since she was a juvenile. Sadly it was inoperable; it was too deep in the thalamus. We found out that the presenting symptoms of an advanced tumour was increased intracranial pressure due to mass effect or hydrocephalus, often with symptoms such as headaches, nausea, vomiting, irritability, ataxia, and possible impairing affects to vision.

However, due to the swelling in the brain caused by the haemorrhaging, Anna would require time to rehabilitate. This was causing pressure mainly as a result of the congealed blood, which would slowly decrease in size. As Anna didn't have any prior symptoms in the period before the tumour haemorrhaged they agreed that she would need to be monitored closely as an outpatient over the next few months, in the hope that she would slowly improve and that her anti-seizure medication would minimise her epilepsy. They were ready to implement the discharge plan.

There was a problem. During this period of hospitalisation, Anna's behaviour had changed. She had become aggressive and walked day and night. It was put down to the pressure in her head, so they gave her medication for these symptoms, too.

We decided, during this time, that Anna should have day passes so that she could enjoy outings and return home as much as possible and walk along the river to feel the fresh air and the warmth of the sunshine away from the sterile environment of the hospital. We also, on one occasion, had her return home overnight. We paid a full-time nurse and took shifts as Anna was awake the whole time. This told us a lot. Something was still not right at all. In our view, Anna was far from ready to come home.

The neurological and neurosurgery team thought otherwise—they felt she was ready to be discharged. I remember the day that the neurosurgeon was doing the rounds with his team, including students. He was saying that 'Anna is right to go home' when Anna literally went for him and I didn't stop her. She was very angry as he just wasn't listening. A few of the staff had to try and release him from Anna's strong grip. I don't think anyone had done that to him before when they were told they could go home. After he composed himself, and I got Anna settled, he asked me to join him in the small waiting room so we could have a chat.

I explained to him that Anna was angry because she was in pain. She was telling him something was still very wrong. He explained that it was more than likely that her recovery would take a long time and to accept that Anna was different and had changed. I didn't accept that at all. I asked him if he'd noticed that Anna's glands were swollen and that her jaw was clenched. My instincts told me that there was something wrong with her jaw or mouth and I asked him if he could organise an x-ray. He explained that neurosurgery 'doesn't do jaws'. I explained that without his support we had no way of knowing how we could settle Anna and that it would be impossible for her to return home in her current agitated state. He realised the seriousness of the situation and graciously agreed to have an x-ray taken to find out if there were other complications causing Anna pain.

That afternoon the result of the x-ray revealed that all her wisdom teeth, from the tumour haemorrhaging, were impacted. No wonder she was walking for twenty-four hours a day. She was in horrific pain.

The next day she was in the operating theatre again having all four wisdom teeth removed.

Lesson 58: Be the custodian of knowledge for your loved ones

You can imagine that by this time Anna was feeling pretty lousy. I remember seeing her swollen face and squinty eyes with a bandage wrapped around her head and jaw. She really looked like she had been hit by a bus. I suspect that's what she felt like too.

We continued to comfort her and stimulate her with her favourite things including feeding her ice-cream and junkets, which had a calming effect on her sore mouth. She was bedridden for a good three days as even lifting her head off the pillow was too painful. Slowly the swelling receded and so did the pain. When she was able to get up, she was calm for the first time since being in hospital. At last she was starting her recovery process.

However, her needs were much higher. She was still awake a lot. We then realised we were faced with the next challenge—finding a suitable place where Anna could rehabilitate to give her the best chance of a full recovery. That was harder than we thought.

Anna was twenty years old. She had been living at home with us until three months ago and now, due to what had happened to her, she required much more support. While the discharge options were being explored, we had day passes approved for Anna so she could enjoy getting out of the hospital. We continued to trial overnight stays at home. From this experience we knew that we would not be able to provide the level of support she required.

The social worker and discharge co-ordinator were asked to assist our family with the next step as Anna's hospital bed was in high demand and, now that she had no further medical needs, she could be discharged as soon as a suitable solution was identified. However, we declared Anna 'homeless' as, from our trials at home, it was clear that we did not have the capacity to support her while she was so ill. They did not believe that Anna required rehabilitation as what had happened to her was life-changing and there was no cure or operation for it.

The only solution that the hospital suggested was that Anna should have an ACAT (Aged Care Assessment Tool) approval which would mean that, if she was successful, she could be placed in an aged-care home. I was horrified. They seemed to favour this option. We were on very different paths. Due to this conflict, I needed to crank up the advocacy and find some innovative solutions—otherwise, I knew that the outcome would be disastrous for Anna.

I approached the respite organisation where Anna had 120 hours of support a year. We used to drop her off at their beautiful old Queenslander in Red Hill and there she would happily interact with the other house mates who were staying overnight. She met lots of nice people and some became her friends over time. Anna enjoyed the visits there. Not only did they provide respite for us, but there was a lovely space for her to be independent and just hang out. She had her own bedroom which was so inviting with the soft décor and the traditional tongue-and-groove walls and pressed-metal ceilings.

I asked whether it was possible to have three months of respite, using our 120 hours in one block period, as well as top-up funding, if I could get it, from Disability Services (for additional personal care support) and the Department of Health (for a full-time nurse for Anna). They were receptive to the idea and had the capacity to do it if we found the funding. So we put forward a proposal to both departments and we were successful. It was approved with three months' emergency funding was made available immediately. You can imagine our relief.

However, there was some organising to be undertaken to find a suitable nurse and also to ensure that the service provider would have the staffing to meet Anna's needs for the three months as it had all happened so fast. So we worked together to make a roster and they were able, miraculously, to find the staff, most of whom Anna knew, so that it was all in place within a week. The nurse we found through the hospital had worked there under an agency and Anna had really liked her. Fortunately she was available and it all fell seamlessly into place.

Anna could then be discharged as we had an option that our family felt would meet her needs and that would enable her to be in a safe, familiar environment, with people she knew and a nurse as a safeguard. She also had an ACAT approval, which the hospital was delighted about—they saw it as a 'blessing' and felt she was very fortunate to get one as they were highly sought after. Although we appreciated their efforts, I am proud to say that the document was carefully filed in a drawer, where it has been ever since, collecting dust.

You could see by Anna's face and her body language that she was happy to be leaving the hospital at last. When we drove her to Red Hill she was also perfectly relaxed as she knew the surroundings and, as we had hoped, she looked pleased to be in her welcoming bedroom that was waiting for her with books, photographs, and lots of her favourite DVDs. I must admit that the first night she was there I also stayed with her, as I was concerned that she would have lots of 'awake time' and, as the nurse didn't really know Anna that well, I preferred to be there. It turned out that Anna's first night was very restless and she had a broken night's sleep. I was pleased I stayed. It gave the nurse a better understanding of Anna's needs and I could see that she was more than capable of supporting Anna from then on, which was reassuring.

Over the three months I took lots of photographs of Anna's progress as evidence of her improvement. It was very gradual. Anna still didn't recognise me as she had lost her memory at the time of the brain haemorrhage. Her memory loss made me feel very sad as it was as though she had gone back into her 'inner world' from when she was a little girl. I was forever hopeful, though, that she would fully recover, so we remained focused on activities that would stimulate her, such as jig-saw puzzles and DVDs of her singing at the Shine concert in the UK, which previously had always made her animated. There was very little response from Anna as she struggled to overcome her condition caused by the haemorrhage. She was also on medication, which caused other side effects that meant her fits—some of which were chronic seizures—were managed. It was at those times that we were so grateful that the nurse was there. I'm convinced that Anna would not have survived during her period of rehabilitation had it not been for the nurse's expertise, as Anna had several chronic episodes that without immediate medical response may have resulted in a very different outcome.

Regardless of her challenges, Anna was still Anna. In my eyes, all that she needed was love, support, and encouragement to return to her former glory. I stayed focused on that goal.

Lesson 59: Focus on the person, not on the medical condition

Just prior to the end of the three months, I could see that Anna needed more time to rehabilitate; although there was improvement, her needs were still very high. My only hope was to submit a further proposal for another month's funding to give Anna the best chance of recovery. It also gave us time to explore other living arrangements for Anna on a medium- to long-term basis.

During this time, Anna continued to come home regularly so that we could see how we would manage on our own. No matter how much we tried, Anna required more support than we could give her. So we knew it was the right decision to begin looking at all the accommodation options for her in the next phase of her life.

Fortunately, the proposal for the extension was approved and during this time there were some good indicators that Anna was starting to come out of her 'inner world' and enjoy some of her hobbies, including painting. One afternoon, I remember vividly, we were painting together and suddenly Anna picked up a tube of paint and gave it to me. She said, "Blue now!" It was a precious moment as not only had Anna recognised the colour and remembered it was blue but she was also, in no uncertain terms, telling me that the terracotta colour I was applying to the background of the painting needed to be blue instead!

I took her advice and went about changing it to blue which, against the white painted flower, looked stunning. She was absolutely right. I recall, too, that it was Anzac Day. To mark the occasion, and to symbolise the pain of

Anna's recent journey, I added red acrylic paint to the image, dripping from the petal on the flower down to the base of its stem. The white flower gave hope and the red contrast was a reminder of loss. It seemed, from both perspectives, very relevant and very real. The framed painting now hangs proudly in our lounge room as a poignant reminder of when Anna's world reunited with ours.

Lesson 60: Art can inspire renewed hope, rejuvenation, and reconnection

There were many happy memories of Anna's continued improvement. By the end of the fourth month Anna transitioned into supported accommodation, where once again I went with my bags packed to stay overnight in her two-bedroom unit. I needed to be sure it was right for her and, although I may have been extreme in my actions, I have no regrets about what I did.

It gave me peace of mind that Anna was being given the right level of care to meet her needs and that she was happy. By day three, I felt the support workers understood Anna's needs and were getting to know her as a person. Anna looked comfortable around them and I knew that I could leave her there safely.

Nonetheless the guilt I had was massive. It was the hardest thing I've ever had to do (other than leave Claire in the UK) as the transition we had planned was that Anna was going to live independently in the downstairs part of a house that we were just about to put a deposit on when she took ill. Everything had changed.

Instead we were grateful that Anna had survived and that she was improving. The four months' rehabilitation plan had worked and at that time a vacancy had become available at Mercy Community Services for a two-bedroom unit adjacent to several other villas where ladies lived together who Anna could visit. She loved having dinner with them and then she would be supported to return to her own home and get ready for bed.

Under her funding package, which was approved every three months, Anna received 1:1 support to meet her personal care needs. The team was encouraged to apply person-centred approaches with Anna by focusing on her strengths. I am grateful for their support and their dedication. We were relieved after several years of having to apply for funding every three months, to have recurrent funding approved. That gave Anna much more stability so it was a good time to explore other accommodation options; in particular, living in the community.

We rented a two-bedroom unit in Mitchelton. This was brand new housing stock through the Department of Housing. It was spacious and had a rear deck that overlooked a park, opposite the local RSL, and with the library and shopping centre nearby. It ticked all the boxes, including having a single-car garage, which was a bonus. We were keen to get her a car so that her support workers could take her out more as she loved going for a drive.

We'd agreed to see if Anna could transition from the supported accommodation to living in the community. We wanted to trial it without risking her losing her place where she lived, so we simply connected her to the community in Mitchelton while we paid rent at both her supported accommodation and at her unit. During this time she registered as a volunteer with some of the local organisations. She also spent time at her new place where she would have afternoon tea and then return to her home at Wooloowin.

The unit at Mitchelton was affordable as it was under social housing and was only a percentage of Anna's pension per week. However, we had to find tenants who would be happy to live with Anna without paying board, in return for a reciprocal arrangement where they would provide the meal at dinner time and allocate some time to Anna during the weekends to take her out. Her personal care needs would be met by support workers who would come in for certain periods during the day and support her at courses and with other activities as well as providing personal care. This concept came from a charity that we established when Anna took ill and she was, for all intents and purposes, homeless, as there were not any suitable options available at that time. We wanted to create a housing model where people were respected and where they had choice in their lifestyle and had control of their decision-making. We were hopeful that if Anna went into supported accommodation, it may just be temporary while we established SMARTCare Lifestyle Solutions Foundation.

It was our hope that Anna, and other young people in similar situations, could, as our slogan said, 'Live with the people of their choice, in the housing of their choice, in the community of their choice'. We had several families that each had the same vision for their sons and daughters; to provide them with independent lifestyles and to ensure that, as part of their succession planning, there were sustainable options that would provide stability and support according to their loved ones' needs even after they were gone. Many of those families found interim solutions based on those principles, which was wonderful.

This model didn't work for Anna, due to her high needs and her cognitive development. It proved difficult to find a couple that was happy to live under the reciprocal arrangement, even with the benefits of being rent-free. When we found a couple that we thought would be perfect, the husband got a transfer to Melbourne. It was after six months of the trial that I realised it wasn't working for Anna. Things weren't falling into place at all. I remember sobbing my heart out, feeling that I had failed. Some years later I realised that I would never have known without trying. It comforted me to know that we had given it a go for six months. Anna had experienced the best of both worlds.

Thanks to that keyhole of trialling living in the community, we identified that Anna would be isolated (as she wasn't adjoined to any villas—instead she was a tenant in a block of units) and that she would be at risk of being unattended at times and living in a setting that wasn't sustainable. It would have required micro-management to ensure it worked well.

Over time, I realised what wonderful knowledge we took from that six-month trial. In fact, there wasn't anything negative about it all—it had told us everything we needed to know during that period and Anna met some wonderful people and became engaged in another community, which was enriching for her.

It also helped me to come to the conclusion that her supported accommodation did meet her needs and that she was happy there. It had taken me a long time to reach that decision as I had carried the burden of guilt for a long time. Now, for the first time, I felt lighter and more at peace with our decision.

Lesson 61: Give it a go—even if it fails, it provides insight and valuable lessons

Over the next seven years Anna was in and out of hospital regularly. Her stamina and determination, along with her strength of character, stood her in good stead each time another obstacle was put in front of her. It was always around October/November each year that Anna was admitted to hospital, usually for months at a time due to her neurological symptoms As other tumours emerged that were operable, they were de-bulked, which improved her mobility and enabled her, after much rehabilitation, to regain her strength. It was remarkable how she went from being in a wheelchair to walking again once she had fully recovered.

During this time she had multiple operations. Anna got pneumonia and was in ICU again and was not expected to live. I recall how I was taken into the grey room and told to expect the worst. Instead I rang a friend. He was a physio and Anna needed as many physios as she could to relieve her of her symptoms of congestion and mucus build-up that were causing her saturation levels to drop dangerously low.

When Nic came, they were already below the level at which it was considered possible to see improvement. We got permission for Nic and me to work alongside the ICU physio. Anna was constantly turned and suctioned and required gentle tapping on her chest. We did that relentlessly for twenty-four hours together. Little by little, we saw improvement. We did it. Anna turned the corner and pulled through, yet again. It was remarkable. I will always be eternally grateful to Nic, who I regard as being Anna's guardian angel that night. Without his help, we know it may have been a very different outcome.

Lesson 62: Ring a friend when you need help

Another time when we sought assistance from a colleague was in 2011, when Anna's medication was starting to cause her long-term problems. This included issues with her bowels and her behaviour. She was becoming easily agitated, and, at her worst, was aggressive. It was the medication, not Anna. She was simply dealing with something over which she had no control. The neurologist at that time didn't believe that the anti-seizure medication was the cause. My instincts told me very differently. The reason I felt so sure is that it was the only thing that had changed over the past year and, in my opinion, that's when the first symptoms occurred and then got progressively worse.

I desperately contacted Professor Harry McConnell, a neuropsychiatrist from St Vincent's Private Hospital, Brisbane, who specialised in rare disabilities and behaviours associated with certain medications. I explained that Anna needed a second opinion and that I was concerned that the medication she was on was not suitable. He suggested that, as he wasn't a visiting doctor at the hospital where Anna was admitted, we should wait until she was discharged to see him as an outpatient. I knew we had no time to waste as Anna was clearly getting more and more stressed and hyperactive. I could see that she was heading for another grand mal seizure, which by this time were becoming more frequent and more dangerous. I explained that something needed to happen urgently and asked if he could weave any magic at his end. I assured him that I would do all I could to help.

What happened next is a blur. Shortly after the phone call, the professor was miraculously sitting with Anna and me in the hospital ward. He was observing her and he was very shocked to see her heightened state of agitation. He asked for her chart and recognised many culprits amongst the concoction of medications. Following that assessment, he gave seven recommendations, including that Anna should slowly be weaned off several of the medications and gradually commence using other more suitable anti-seizure medications that were compatible with her condition. Professor McConnell worked in consultation with Anna's neurologist so that Anna could start improving. Her behaviour returned to normal. However, her bowels never did recover, and it required a life-long, dedicated regime to ensure her regularity.

I was so grateful for the knowledge and wise advice of Professor McConnell, who was integral to improving Anna's quality of life by overseeing her medications and her end of life 'Statement of Views' (more commonly known as an Advance Care Plan) that enabled Anna to express her wishes, which were honoured.

Lesson 63: Source specialists who understand your condition

Although Anna's anti-seizure medications improved her behaviour, she was still having seizures and headaches when she would rub her head. She was starting to be very unwell—it was another bad patch and she was hospitalised again. By this time, Anna not only had the astrocytoma, she had several meningiomas in her brain that were also benign. However, they were fast-growing, and to relieve her hydrocephalus caused and exacerbated by the multiple tumours they inserted a shunt. She was twenty-six years old.

The operation was successful and Anna was given the nod of approval to go home. The shunt provided her with relief from headaches and improved her seizure activity, which had over the previous few years become worse. Anna would often go into trances prior to having petit mal seizures and would be admitted to hospital regularly to review her anti-seizure medication so that she could become stable again. She would also be hospitalised for treatment for her chronic constipation that was caused, in large part, by the medication.

Anna was re-admitted to hospital after an x-ray revealed that her colon was permanently damaged. This news was another big blow to us as it impacted on her quality of life from then on.

In that same year I recall breaking the rules again when I noticed, as Anna got up, that she was unsteady on her feet. It looked to me like she was a drunken sailor. Although we were in the neurology ward, I had the neurosurgeon's mobile number (as you do!) in my phone so I called him, not expecting him to answer the phone. Much to my relief, he did. Once I had told him Anna's symptoms he rushed over to the ward as he was nearby. He assessed Anna, then looked at his operating schedule and explained that he had one space the following day where he could undertake a procedure to de-bulk the tumour. From the recent MRI scans they knew its size and its location and that, at some point, it would start impacting on Anna's mobility due to its position in her cerebellum. I checked with Anna first and she gave consent.

I then met with the neurosurgeon's registrar who explained the risks and took me through what the operation entailed. He confirmed the urgency and that the risks were high. My feelings were that if Anna didn't have the operation it would not be long before she was back in hospital with a broken limb or something worse. I'm pleased to say that the operation went well. They were not able to remove the entire tumour, as it was too close to her brain stem. However, it was reduced enough to immediately improve Anna's mobility and, after several months of rehabilitation, she was back to her old self and walking as robustly and purposefully as ever.

I also remember the surprise of the staff in the neurological ward that day that the neurosurgeon could have come to visit Anna without going through the internal referral process. He had just appeared, given his assessment, and booked Anna in for an operation within twenty-four hours. I explained that I had built trust in and a connection with him and that Anna had also left her mark on him since that day when she literally threw herself at him in rage when it was subsequently discovered that she had four impacted wisdom teeth. So I suppose we did have a history together.

The silos, with each ward operating in its own area (which I had witnessed in the medical system when Anna was first admitted to hospital six years earlier), were starting to become less evident. The staff were listening more and I felt that they were providing patients who had cognitive learning development more consideration and respect. It was both reassuring and comforting to see the changes occurring that were so important for ensuring the best outcome for the patient. I was very grateful for the immediate response that day, when the neurosurgeon had seen Anna's vulnerability and was able to make a difference and improve Anna's quality of life. His selfless actions gave Anna back her independence and dignity.

> *Lesson 64: Break the rules—do whatever it takes to improve the situation*

Chapter 8
Life-Changing Decisions

Each operation that Anna had impacted on her overall health. By twenty-seven years of age she required thickened fluids and pureed food as her lungs had been affected by both pneumonia and anaesthetic. This, along with her bowel routine, was just a natural part of her life for two years. Anna could still enjoy her thick shakes and cappuccinos, to which we simply added thickener. In fact, every time I ordered a coffee I would ask for extra froth as I knew that Anna would, often when I was not looking, take a spoonful of mine just because she could! It made me laugh. And, to this very day, anyone who goes out for coffee with me knows I still order extra froth. It's become a tradition.

The last operation that Anna had was nothing to do with neurology or neurosurgery. She had a tumour in the base of her right foot. This was extremely painful as it had caused the nerve endings to twist around themselves, leading to the formation of a growth in the exact position where she would weight-bear when she walked.

Although the tumour was not life-threatening, it was impacting on Anna's quality of life. After much consultation it was agreed that if Anna didn't have the tumour removed, her mobility would be compromised and, as it was fast-growing, this could mean she would be in a wheelchair before long as the pain would be too great for her to walk. It was another tough decision, particularly knowing that her lungs were weak. However, they reassured us that they could manage her breathing under the anaesthetic as they were aware of her delayed swallowing and weak lungs and would take the necessary precautions. After weighing it all up, and explaining to Anna what her options were, we agreed to proceed.

It was a very difficult time for her, as although Anna got through the operation, it took a toll on her in several ways. She seemed to have reached a point where she'd had enough. I even saw her with a tear in her eye one day, and, for Anna, who I never saw cry, that told me everything. And then she said, "No more." I listened and I fully respected her wishes and agreed that if she felt that way, enough was enough. Over the six weeks that followed, Anna didn't get any happier. She sat slumped in her wheelchair, disengaged. They expected that her recovery would mean she could walk on her foot again and that she would resume her normal routine, but something had changed. Several people, including Anna's GP, said at that time that I should expect the worst as Anna was most likely nearing the end of her life and that I needed to prepare myself.

I asked myself how I could improve her wellness and enable her to return to her happy-go-lucky self. I wasn't giving up. She needed help. So I ignored the GP who said to accept the status quo. Instead I asked him for a referral to a specialist at the Queensland Pain Clinic that had a reputation for being person-centred and innovative in his approach. That's what Anna needed—someone who could think outside of the box.

I recall our first appointment vividly. Anna was depressed and sitting forlornly in her wheelchair, with no interest whatsoever in anything. She was back in her 'inner world'. He looked at Anna and said, "Well, young lady, you don't look at all happy. Let's see if we can change that!" He did an examination and gleaned that Anna had neuropathic pain down her neck, back, and arms. He gave her an ointment to apply three times a day, to numb those areas, so that she would not be able to feel the neuropathic pain. The pain specialist also gave her a tablet for pain relief, too. He told us that Panadol, which Anna had been taking every four hours, would simply not touch the neuropathic pain. No wonder Anna was miserable.

We returned a month later. Anna was out of the wheelchair and chatting away in the waiting room. When the pain specialist saw her, he had a smile from ear to ear. His treatment had indeed worked. Anna was relieved of her symptoms and was able to return to feeling pain-free—her life was good again.

That day, we went down to the old tree that stands in the grounds of the hospital by the river. I asked a passer-by to take a photograph of us together. I stretched my arms up to the sky to show my gratitude that Anna's pain-management had given her relief. We made a pact that day, a pact that changed us both forever, that we would enjoy life to the fullest and that the word 'palliative' would not exist in our vocabulary. (It didn't for Anna anyway!) The words 'hope' and 'fun' became part of our mantra. It showed in our faces in the photograph from that day. The photo acts as a poignant reminder of how we embraced living in the present and celebrating what we had.

Lesson 65: Live in the present, celebrate the now

Over the following eighteen months Anna and I lived from the heart. We went to places for long weekends; sometimes at my own peril. One such time was when we went to Caloundra and stayed at a beautiful unit overlooking the Pumicestone Passage. It wasn't the one we had owned that towered above Bribie Island. This one was on the ground floor, where you could literally hang a fishing line out over the rails—that's how close we were to the water! It was so peaceful and it had an open plan whereby you could look out from the lounge room and watch the boats go by. Knowing Anna's love for boats, it seemed perfect. It also had a large spa right in the middle of the unit.

My first mistake was to think that Anna was still strong enough to get in and out of the spa. I found this out very quickly after a wonderful hour watching *Midsomer*

Murders from the comfort of the hot, bubbly spa. It was just so special, both of us indulging in the spa, watching television (which was positioned perfectly on the wall opposite the spa), and watching the boats and pelicans go past. I had also cut Anna's hair just before we had a spa, as I loved styling and shaping her thick, black hair that grew so quickly. It was just such a delight to pamper her and she always looked so happy after I had done it. To have a haircut that day, followed by just hanging out together, was really heavenly and it was fun. It was in keeping with our mantra.

As I tried to get Anna out of the spa, I realised that she couldn't move. Her oedema was causing swelling in her ankles and legs but she was literally stuck in a cross-legged position, as that's how she had been sitting in the spa. Now I weigh fifty-two kilograms and Anna was somewhat heavier than me, with a larger frame. I had to remain calm and be innovative. So I tried all the usual approaches, like coaxing her out with an ice-cream. That didn't work. Then I tried a few physical techniques, such as putting my arms under hers and levering her up. That didn't work either. I stopped and put a towel around her, dried the bath with a towel so that it wasn't slippery, and made us both a cuppa to gather my thoughts and look like I was totally in control of the situation. I came to the conclusion that, if all else failed, I would make a bed for us both in the spa and seek help the next morning.

With that option firmly planted in my head, I was more relaxed. I told Anna everything was going to be fine. From the look in her eyes, I knew she wasn't convinced.

We had our cuppas and resumed where we had left off. Still no luck.

I was about to go into Plan B mode and put pillows and blankets in the spa when I accidentally hit the tap, causing the hot water to gush out. That made Anna move and, quick as a flash, I grabbed her and spun her out of the bath before she got scalded. Well, I hadn't thought of that one in my plan—I guess that's a good thing really!

However in my exuberance I hadn't noticed that the bed, which was nearby, had wooden feet that protruded out from the base. Somehow I managed to hit it with my big toe as I swung Anna out of the spa on to firm ground. Much to my horror, my toenail came off. The whole night was a bit like *Fawlty Towers.* Anna started to chuckle, seeing me jumping up and down like I was doing an Indian war-dance. I was in excruciating pain. Anna then started to laugh heartily. I realised that she saw the funny side of it and was extremely amused by my antics. I'm quite sure she thought it was payback for having hot water poured on her.

The next morning, my toe wounded and my pride dented, I felt vulnerable and tired. At first Anna was oblivious to the fact that I was exhausted. I hadn't slept much. Then Anna turned toward me on the beach and took my hand with her clenched fist as she realised I was struggling. She gave me the strength to revitalise and to appreciate how special our bond was—I felt her love topping up my energy. We were back on track—Mum and daughter walking on the beach, hand-in-hand, with not a care in the world.

Lesson 66: Appreciate that tough times can make the good times seem so much better

While we were having all these colourful adventures and just hanging out, we also decided, while Anna was in a good space, to start planning for the end of her life. It was important that her wishes should be honoured when the time came. The problem was that a Care Directive was not legally binding if it wasn't signed by the person or if they couldn't read it. Other than recognising the word 'omelette', Anna's reading and comprehension was limited.

I was fortunate that Professor McConnell, who was overseeing Anna's medications and who was aware of the dilemma in our quest to find a way for Anna to express her wishes, contacted me. He asked if Anna and I would like to come into his office and meet with the team, who were keen to talk with us about creating such a document. We were elated.

Anna was the first person through the Health Advocacy Legal Clinic (HALC) at St Vincent's Private Hospital, Brisbane, in partnership with the Queensland Public Interest Law Clearing House Incorporated (QPILCH) who created a 'Statement of Views', otherwise known as an Advance Care Plan. HALC and QPILCH had been successful in receiving a small grant to assist people with a disability or other challenges with legal matters.

The first part of the four-page document showed a beautiful photo of Anna on the front and talked about her passions, hobbies, likes, and dislikes. The second part, which took over twelve months to compile, comprised her answers to various questions as to what she would want if her health declined. It was done in a very caring and gentle way and, as I say, over a period of time where it was just happening behind the scenes.

The team would give me a set of questions and when Anna was home I would ask her for her response. I would draw a picture or ask it in a simple way. It worked. Anna fully understood what we were doing. She was very clear when I asked her about what was important to her if it ever got to a point that she wasn't going to get better—living a long life or having a shorter life that focused on her comfort and care? She wanted the latter. She also wanted people who loved her to be with her in her own home. She wanted to have visitors—but not too many as she disliked crowds. She wanted to have flowers and bright and lovely things around her. She wanted to enjoy outings in her blue Holden Astra that she loved.

We gave the car to Anna on her 27th birthday so that her devoted support workers could chauffeur her around wherever she wanted. Buying that car was one of the best things we ever did. It gave her independence, and like any young adult, she had her own wheels, along with cool tinted windows and a rear spoiler.

The document also listed Anna's multi-disciplinary teams, spread across several hospitals and covering neurologists, neuropsychiatrists, neurosurgeons, gastroenterologists, and the clinician who was recording a holistic case study of Anna's medical history. It was the first time on any document that I had seen her swag of doctors, specialists, and clinicians in one list, together with all their contact details. It was invaluable.

Anna also asked that her service celebrating her life should be focused on community rather than religion. I was actually surprised where that could have come from. I didn't know she thought that! It was simply through asking the questions that we found out what Anna wanted, right down to that important detail.

> Lesson 67: Prepare for end of life by honouring your loved one's wishes with integrity

We were able to share Anna's Statement of Views with the hospitals and her GPs as well as with her support team. A copy was kept in her blue medical folder. Any time Anna was visiting her specialists they would be aware of it and, of course, if an ambulance had to be called, then they too would see the document in her folder. It was a safeguard. It gave Anna control of her decision-making and her future. She knew that, through that process, she had shared the vital bits of information that we would not otherwise have known. It gave me peace of mind.

So with that job done we continued to enjoy ourselves until, one day at the end of February 2015, I was out with friends farewelling a special work colleague when I got a phone call from Anna's support worker explaining that Anna had collapsed and wasn't able to walk.

I went immediately to Anna's place and saw that she was extremely unwell. I popped her in the wheelchair, which was always on hand, and brought her home. She loved her bedroom and staying overnight on weekends, for special celebrations, or when she was unwell. It overlooked a courtyard where she could sit in the sun and have privacy and often paint. Her room was filled with light and her own beautiful masterpieces hung on the walls.

> *Lesson 68: Surroundings that are welcoming and safe provide peace and comfort*

The last time Anna came home to stay was for Christmas, a few months earlier. She usually loved our time together. However, she shocked me by grabbing her car keys within hours of arriving on Christmas Eve, insisting that she wanted to go home. She didn't care that no-one was at her place (as her devoted team were on holidays) and that our neighbours were putting on a barbecue because they knew that Anna was coming home for Christmas. It was tricky. Mind you, it also told me that she was happy with her independent living and with her own place, which was comforting to me.

However, when Anna was undiplomatic it was a challenge as she was also very stubborn. Eventually I convinced her that she couldn't go back to her place. It turned out that she just didn't want to go to the barbecue—there were too many people. I had forgotten her dislike for crowds.

Realising why she was restless, I apologised and said that we would not be joining them. They were kind enough to bring up a plate of food for us both. Anna made it clear from her actions that she was grateful but wanted to be left alone with her Mum. So we ate together on the front deck, watching everyone else enjoy their lunch down by the pool. That was Anna. She was starting to relax by the evening so we watched *Midsomer Murders* together, which was now our favourite show. We loved counting how many people died—this kept Anna amused, particularly if there were more than three. We often joked, too, that we wouldn't live in Midsomer!

The following day, Anna was more receptive, as there was so much going on with presents to open, helping Colin cook the roast turkey, and enjoying a lovely three-course meal. After lunch we went on the City Hopper to where she hoped the café, to which we went regularly, would be open (as she was keen to have her cappuccino and the froth from mine). Of course it was closed. Anna, unperturbed by this fact, set on a course to go to the restaurant that was filled with people having their prolonged Christmas lunches.

The waitress was stressed and, when we came in, it escalated. She spoke quickly and told us that we couldn't reasonably expect a table unless we had booked. Fair enough. Anna saw that as a 'no' and then walked purposefully out to find another café that would oblige.

I followed her as she was powerwalking and I had to run to catch up to her. I heard footsteps behind us and someone singing out to us. It was the manager of the café who apologised for the behaviour of his staff member and asked what we wanted. Anna did the sign for a drink. He explained that he would make a table available for us for high tea, which would be on the house. That was impressive.

It made me smile when we were eating our scones with our cappuccinos (with extra froth!) on the white-starched linen tablecloth while we overlooked the Story Bridge. We were so blessed that day, as little did we know then that his random act of kindness would be a precious memory. That was our last Christmas with Anna.

Lesson 69: Practise random acts of kindness, they bring joy and happiness

Anna had now been home a few days since she collapsed and her symptoms were worsening. We had made a pact that I would phone for the ambulance if she wasn't improving. She was resting in bed and not drinking any thickened fluids. Her appetite was reasonable but I knew that she was struggling. She agreed that it was time to go to the hospital for an assessment and she was very co-operative when the ambos popped her onto the stretcher. Upon being seen in emergency, Anna consented to having a CAT scan.

For me, it was another huge realisation. Six months earlier, I had collapsed when I was having an x-ray and the nurses thought it was very odd. My white cell blood count had been consistently under the normal range over the past year and I was being monitored. I was sent off for further tests, including a bone marrow biopsy, which confirmed that I had Chronic Lymphocytic Leukaemia (CLL).

They believe the radiation over the years from when I had gone with Anna into her scans and x-rays may have triggered the condition, along with my gene mutation. Fortunately I was in the early stages. I was grateful that it had been detected early, as just as I had done with Anna, I worked with both the medical professionals and with complementary therapists to enhance my wellness. That's why I had blood tests regularly to improve my thyroid condition. Over the years, and with the help of Bach flower remedies, my goitre disappeared and my thyroid levels returned to normal. It had worked.

I would approach my newly-found early diagnosis in exactly the same way. The only thing I added to my routine was having more alkaline food and water in my diet and, most importantly, not exposing myself to further radiation. My daily exercise regime on my rebounder (small trampoline) where I gently bounce for ten minutes in the morning and in the evening helps with strengthening my core muscles and improves my lymph drainage, along with doing five minutes of integrated movement therapy that helps with co-ordination and balancing the left and right-hand side of my brain.

Lesson 70: Take control of your health with regular check-ups and natural therapies

For the first time, I was now faced with the reality that I couldn't join Anna for her scan. If I did, I would collapse again. I phoned friends. I was grateful for their support and help. They were able to be there for Anna at her time of need. I waited outside anxiously as I felt helpless and realised that both Anna and I were vulnerable.

Lesson 71: Allow yourself to be vulnerable

Anna's scan results revealed that the tumour that had previously been de-bulked had grown back aggressively. A further large meningioma had also appeared and was equally aggressive. Both were in her cerebellum, thereby causing her to have mobility issues, which explained why she had collapsed. Over and above these two large tumours, she also had numerous other meningiomas, some of which were small and others were medium-sized. The astrocytoma tumour that had originally haemorrhaged now had a cluster of smaller tumours around it.

When the doctor came into the room, his face said it all. He clearly had some grave news. I sought Anna's consent for me to step out of the room and look at the scan as the doctor felt he could then explain it to me.

When I saw the scan, I was horrified. How could so many tumours have multiplied in such a short space of time? The doctor explained that Anna would need to be admitted to hospital while decisions were made as to how we would proceed. Although Anna had made a decision eighteen months earlier to have no further medical intervention and she had her Statement of Views, we needed to give her options for her to be in control.

I returned to the cubicle where Anna looked at me with her trusting eyes and I asked if she would agree to stay for a short time in the hospital while we found out how we could make her feel better. She consented willingly.

Over the days that followed, Anna had her ups and downs. When she was good, she enjoyed painting and sitting on the chair next to her bed, propped up with her paints and canvases. On other days she just rested. During this period the neurosurgery team explained to Anna that she could have an operation on the two large tumours. However, as they had both grown fast in places where they could only be de-bulked, rather than removed, the team were uncertain how much time she would have before she would require another operation. Then, of course, she had twenty or more others growing rapidly too.

The second option was in-home palliative care. As Anna and I did not use the word 'palliative' as it didn't exist in our vocabulary, this option was explained as resting at home and doing as much as she felt she could on any given day with pain management and making her comfortable.

I asked both teams to come into see Anna separately and explain to her in simple terms each of the options. After they had left the room, I grabbed a piece of paper and a pen and drew a circle with a smiley face with Anna's name written on the top of the page.

In the middle of the smiley face I wrote '1—operation' and '2—rest at home'. I then asked Anna, in a non-biased way, which option she would prefer. It would have been so easy for me to make the second option more appealing, simply with my voice intonation. I was very mindful of how I spoke. I gently explained how an operation may give her some improvement and also may give her more time. Whether it would be quality time was uncertain. The second option of resting at home meant that, according to the doctors and without the operation, Anna would have approximately two months to live. She could return to her own home or mine and go to sleep and one day she wouldn't wake up.

I checked in with how she was going. She was totally present. She pointed to the second option and said, with great purpose, "Good." I then reworded the questions so that I was absolutely sure she knew what it meant. She confirmed that she definitely understood and I stepped out to the corridor to beckon the doctor back in.

I couldn't talk, nor could I go back in to Anna until I was composed. He was so kind and gentle. He had been on Anna's journey for over six years and I recall fondly that Anna had a special place for him in her heart. One year she had celebrated her 25th birthday while she was in hospital and he had seen her dressed up and looking absolutely beautiful. She turned on the charm that day.

Here we were, four years on, facing a very different scenario. After composing myself, the compassionate doctor and I walked into Anna's room. He said to Anna that he felt she had made the right decision and that he would call the palliative care team and ask them to speak with her. He was very supportive and I could feel his sadness too as he knew that Anna was such a fighter and that fighting now may prove to be the greatest challenge of her life.

The palliative care team explained that Anna could be discharged after her pain management was reviewed so that it improved her quality of life. It was then that I pulled out Anna's Statement of Views, which outlined exactly what she wanted. The team were so grateful that Anna had prepared for this moment. The statement confirmed Anna's decision and it meant they could proceed with certainty. It was such a blessing having the document that became integral to ensuring Anna's end of life journey was made easier and that she was in control of her destiny.

Lesson 72: Clarify the person's wishes and give them control

Chapter 9
Honouring

Anna was discharged a week after she had been admitted to the hospital. As she required such a high level of care, I asked if she was fine with coming home with me for the first week and then we would review it. She was happy with that plan.

During the next week, her devoted team of Kathy, Olivia, and Beth worked eight-hour shifts and would come in every day chirpy and bright. Each brought their own gifts, their own style. Anna loved them all and responded differently to each of them. Olivia was like another sister to Anna and they had a special bond, particularly working closely with one another for many years; Kathy made Anna smile a lot and I'd find the two of them chuckling in her room while they were playing a game or reading or watching a DVD. They had fun. Beth, who came one day a week, was like a breath of fresh air and she would simply breeze in and be sensitive and caring and always seem to know exactly what Anna needed. Then she would seamlessly breeze out again. By the end of the first week Anna made it very clear, when Kathy took her out for a drive to her place that she wanted to come back to her mum's home. In fact, Kathy and Anna were both very solemn when they returned with Anna sulking in her wheelchair with her white panama hat on and her black, yellow, and orange sarong across her lap. She didn't look happy. Kathy explained that she wouldn't take Anna back to her place again as it was clear Anna preferred being with her mum now. I thought it was wonderful. It told me exactly what Anna wanted and I was very happy.

Every day was different. There were many precious moments. There were times where no words were said—we were silent and shared a sacred space. Daily meditation music and massages, along with her outings and visits by friends, gave Anna joy.

Her condition progressed and the medication to ease her pain was increased, and she rested more. She was calm and, for the first time, due to the large doses of clonazepam, Anna could do things she had never done before, like hold my hand in a cupped and loving way. Previously it was always with her knuckles tightly squeezed in. It was wonderful seeing her long fingers and feeling her hand in mine. Toward the end she would want me to hold her hand when one of her devoted team pushed her wheelchair and I walked beside as though we were one. We were.

She also surprised us one day when Kathy was making Anna's favourite avocado meal. Anna went to the fridge (on this particular day she was able to walk) and got out the parmesan cheese. Kathy explained to her that it was the wrong one and to put it back and get the mature cheese. Anna put it back, as she was told, and then took out the parmesan again. We both chuckled. Anna knew exactly what she wanted. What we hadn't expected was that as Kathy was slicing the avocado and I was thickening a jug of water, Anna got a knife and cut a big wedge of the parmesan and stuck it in her mouth. It was hilarious. Of course, the fact that it could have choked her and she could have cut her finger wasn't funny, but the act of sheer determination and independence spoke volumes about the space she was in where she was centred and focused. It was a precious moment that both Kathy and I fondly remember.

It was also during the several months that Anna was home that I was very ill one evening with food poisoning. It's the sickest I've ever been and the ambulance had to be called. Poor Anna. I'm not sure what she thought as she heard her mother being ill and then needing help. Fortunately, the needles they gave me to settle my symptoms worked and I improved over the following hours. However, the next morning, when I would ordinarily have gone in to Anna very early to check on her, instead I watched her on the baby monitor from my bedroom as I was too weak to get up. Anna sang out to me, "Mummy are you alright?" It was so touching. I had never heard her express her concern and love for me in the way she did that day.

When Kathy arrived, she took Anna out in the wheelchair for a walk along the river and to New Farm Park. When they returned, they found me in bed, exhausted. Anna sang out, "Mum!" again, as though checking on me—our roles had reversed for a day. The next thing was that Anna got out of her wheelchair and came and sat on my bed. She brought me flowers that they had picked on their walk. Normally, due to the fact that Anna's fine motor skills were limited, she would find it difficult to hand them to me. With her newfound muscle relaxant, she was able to carefully give me the flowers until they were safely in my hands. I stared at what I had just witnessed. It touched my soul. It was such a beautiful act of love.

Lesson 73: When you show your vulnerability, you let others in

During those months, there were many precious moments where we cherished the time we had together. Kathy, Olivia, and Beth were part of the family. We all knew naturally what to do and how to give Anna the support she needed, each showering her with their love.

Colin would also come and sit with Anna and they had so many quiet and heartfelt moments together, often with neither of them moving. They were still and peaceful.

I would regularly read through Anna's Statement of Views to make sure I was honouring her wishes and I felt comforted to know that they were all being respected. Even when I met with the minister to prepare for Anna's Sacred Sunflower Service, we referred to it as the basis of our meaningful and heartfelt conversation. The clarity it gave us set us straight on the path of a service focused on connecting Anna's communities and celebrating her life.

Two of her wishes were to have visitors and to enjoy outings. I recall fondly the day, a week before Easter, when I picked up a friend from the airport who had come to see Anna and hadn't seen her since she was six years old. As I drove him from the airport to the café, where Anna and Olivia were waiting for us near the Story Bridge and where we came regularly, I explained that Anna was having a good day and that his visit was timely.

It was wonderful that when we arrived Anna greeted us both as though everything was perfectly normal. She looked beautiful and was bright and chirpy. She was wearing her white panama hat and a purple top with her black, yellow, and orange sarong over her lap, looking every bit my brilliant blue bohemian butterfly. No-one would have ever guessed, looking at her, that she was ill.

He smiled as he saw a young, vivacious woman who was holding court and being slightly flirtatious. She loved being out, she loved being with friends. She was in her element. Anna realised that she could amuse us by grabbing the table number, which was a playing card—the six of hearts. It wobbled when you moved the base. Anna seized the moment of having a captive audience and she picked it up and passed it to Olivia. Then the game began. For a good ten minutes the six of hearts was being used like a pawn in a chess game—each person chose to give it to another and it made its way around the table many times, getting more wobbly as it was passed around to each player, each of whom was keen to participate. Anna started to giggle as she saw the funny side of the card flopping from side to side. Then she laughed heartily. We all laughed with her. It was so beautiful that none of us had a care in the world. We were in the moment.

The day continued as it had started, with Anna continuing to enjoy our company and soak up all the attention. We left the café under the big fig tree, where we had been sitting outside in the sunshine immersed in our own bubble, and walked through the park and under the bridge to the Holman Street Terminal. A ferry had just arrived and Anna declared loudly, "Boat now," giving us the message that she was keen to board. Off we went, with another beautiful ten minutes of Anna singing and chatting away as though she'd been given a happy pill. It was simply wonderful to watch. We had lunch at a café at Riverside and that was the day that Anna pointed to the word 'omelette'—she was on fire that day.

The following one was just as amazing. She had reverted to her old self with so much to say and was clearly showing her absolute love for life. She wanted to take our friend on the boat and she was in command of how far we went. Our journey took us to the end of the line at North Shore, Hamilton, where we had never been before. Kathy was with us that day when we disembarked from the City Cat and walked along the promenade. Suddenly, as we got to the end of the path, it forked into a half-circle. Anna got up out of her wheelchair, took my hand, and we walked together as we had done for many years when she powerwalked. She walked with me, confidently and resolutely, following the path around until she took me back to her wheelchair. We were all amazed.

Lesson 74: Rejoice in the unexpected pleasures of life

That night, after our special visitor had gone, I saw Anna change. It's as though she had put every ounce of energy into those two last days. She had performed, giggled, laughed, and been flirtatious. She had walked, gone out for an a la carte lunch on the river, and embraced a mind game, proving me wrong when I thought the card at the café the previous day was a seven of diamonds when Anna had said it was the six of hearts. Olivia had turned the card around and there, on the other side, the side that Anna was looking at, was the six of hearts.

Now she was exhausted and needed rest after such a wonderful weekend. It was clear that something neurological had happened to her as she was sitting on the lounge before she went to bed. She was never the same after that. It was as though she had experienced a cathartic moment when she was blissfully in her absolute glory. She had experienced every ounce of her soul being joyful before she started slipping away.

The week that followed confirmed my fears that Anna's condition had progressed significantly. By Easter Sunday, Anna was taken to hospital as I could no longer comfort her with the pain medication at home. I explained to her that we would just go in to have a review and that it would make her more comfortable. She was too weak to care as she hadn't eaten or drunk for forty-eight hours.

It was uncertain whether Anna would improve, so it was a waiting game for the next few hours. She was not interested in anything. Olivia and I, after the doctor had left us in the private room, decided to take things into our own hands. Both of us had the same idea. Anna's favourite thing was a shower and massage so we managed to get her into her wheelchair and take her into the bathroom. Because it was Easter Sunday, I had bought three sets of bunny ears in with us (as one does!). They were kind of cute as one ear stood up straight and the other one flopped down. There was one pair for Anna, one pair for Olivia, and one for me.

Anna wasn't that interested, which was perfectly understandable, but it seemed like a good idea when I had bought them a week earlier when she was so bright and bubbly. Nonetheless, they were there to be worn, so Olivia and I prepared to give Anna a shower. We looked rather strange in our plastic aprons and Easter bunny ears. It was a good ten minutes into Anna's shower and massage when I had an idea.

I went out and looked in the hospital bag that I had packed earlier. Yes, there it was—Anna's big chocolate Easter egg with bright red foil wrapped around it, making it look so tempting. I took it into the bathroom and squatted on the floor on a towel, just below where Anna was having her shower and massage. I hadn't realised that my bunny ear was tickling Anna in the face as I was so focused on slamming the egg on the floor so that it would shatter into small pieces. Anna giggled. I looked up and I realised what had happened and that I had tickled her face as well as tickled her fancy. I suppose seeing your mother on the floor in a plastic apron, with bunny ears, breaking a chocolate Easter egg would be quite amusing! It felt perfectly normal to me. Anything that would make Anna giggle was a miracle and it made me so happy. I then placed the small bits of chocolate in my hand and held them up close to her face. She carefully took a piece and devoured it. Then the next and the next until she was trying to grab my ring off my finger, thinking it was a piece of chocolate. I went to work and got more pieces until there were none left.

The combination of the shower, massage, chocolate Easter egg, and being tickled by a bunny ear did the trick. When she came out of the bathroom she wanted to stay in her wheelchair and go around the ward as though everything was back to normal. It was just incredible. We left the hospital the following morning after she had had several good-sized meals and her meds had been reviewed so that she was comfortable again.

We never told the staff what had turned Anna around. I guess it's not listed in their options, as we simply focused on what made Anna happy. I'm convinced that Anna truly had nine lives, as her ability to bounce back was phenomenal, based on her will to live and knowing what was important to her. The other ingredient was love. It was love that brought her back that day. It wasn't medication or pain relief, it was pure, unconditional love that both Olivia and I gave to Anna with all our hearts. She felt it, she responded to it, and it pulled her through. That day we witnessed it with our own eyes.

Lesson 75: Be daring and resourceful and take control of the situation

The following week was unpredictable and Blue Nurses, who provided excellent in-home nursing support, and the caring in-home palliative care doctor were coming more regularly. Again I found that the pain management regime at home wasn't offering Anna enough comfort, so we returned to hospital, hoping that it would be like Anna's overnight stay at Easter when her meds were reviewed and she came home.

It became clear that Anna required more care and more pain relief each day until she drifted into a coma two days later. She was peaceful. She could hear, so I encouraged everyone to talk to her as normal and to appreciate the importance of connecting with her as the end of her time on this Earth was getting closer.

To show how much love people had for Anna, several offered to come in and say their goodbyes and also sing and perform for her. She heard her favourite tunes, Fiona with her flute, and Fiona's twins singing 'Oranges and Lemons' and all the other songs that Anna loved. She also had meditational music playing while our young neighbour danced and sang. It was so beautiful. Anna passed away that night peacefully. Colin was by her side.

Anna had made it very clear to me by attempting to pass away twice in that week, that as soon as I was present she would regain her strength and her medical observations (blood pressure, pulse, and breathing) would improve. The nursing staff had never seen anything like it. I realised that both Anna and I were so connected that she really wouldn't pass away in my presence.

When I entered the room, my first words to Colin were, "Anna chose the right person to be with her when she left this Earth." I then went over to Anna, who looked so peaceful, and said, "Well done. I am just so proud of you!"

Lesson 76: Celebrate life to the end

Anna's Sacred Sunflower Service on 22 April was indeed a celebration of her life. Over 130 guests packed the church to pay their respects. Many wore blue, Anna's favourite colour.

The service celebrated all facets of her life and acknowledged that she made a difference to the world. It connected her diverse communities who were able to show their joy and their sadness, and most of all their love.

Olivia read out the following heartfelt poem that she had written so beautifully in dedication to Anna:

> Don't think of her as gone away
> Her journey's just begun
> Life holds so many facets
> This Earth is only one
>
> Just think of her as resting
> From the sorrows and the tears
> In a place of warmth and comfort
> Where there are no days and years
>
> Think how she must be wishing
> That we could know today
> How nothing but our sadness
> Can really pass away
>
> And think of her as living
> In the hearts of those she touched
> For nothing loved is ever lost
> And she was loved so much

Anna's service was a fitting tribute for a woman who had beaten all the odds, who had never given up, who had determination and stamina in bucket-loads and a pure, unconditional love that touched our hearts forever.

As Claire was not able to come from the UK, she planted a beautiful rose in her back garden that has since bloomed profusely and stretches high to the sky. It is an affirmation every day that Anna is happy and Claire remembers her sister when she smells the sweet rose scent and looks at the prolific buds opening into full bloom. These are a reminder of the beauty Anna brought to the world.

Lesson 77: A fitting tribute to celebrate a loved one's life helps with grieving

The days following Anna's passing were very difficult. I was grateful for our family and friends who had shown their support in our time of need. Special friends came from Victoria and from New Zealand to give their love and condolences during our grieving. It was lovely to share precious time with them so that we could share our pain together. It helped tremendously.

The day when I was most disorientated was 17 April, the day after Anna had passed away. It felt surreal. Everything was the same, but nothing was the same.

I walked around peacefully but without purpose. I recall that the hi-lo bed that had been loaned to us was being collected and I had to get the sheets off the bed quickly as he was about to arrive. I threw them in the washing machine as my heart ached too much and I knew if I paused and thought about what was happening I would break down and cry.

Just at this point when I felt total loss, the front door buzzer rang. I thought it would be the man to pick up the bed. To my surprise it was Olivia who would have been on duty that day. She wanted to check in on me. I was so grateful to hear her voice. I let her in and we hugged one another and we decided that we would carry on as if Anna was still around. She helped me in more ways than she realised that day. Sure, the fact that when she went into the laundry and opened the washing machine to find wads of gluggy, tissue-like paper thickly covering the washed sheets and told me not to enter the room but to hand her the vacuum so she could vacuum my washing machine out, was extremely helpful. I believe I would have lost it had I seen the mess. It was just the fact that she cared. We were both displaced and both needed one another.

She was there because she was feeling the loss as much as I was. We had been a team, and we were still a team. In the afternoon, when we reflected on our day, the door buzzer went again.

This time it was Kathy just checking in to see how I was. I explained that Olivia was with me and that we'd love it if she joined us. I remember her words: "I'm not here. I'm just checking in." Just as well I ignored her first sentence as she was very much there and Olivia and I were so happy to see her. Not long after that, the door buzzer went again. This time it was Maryanne from work—just checking in on me. We decided then to just chill and chat when the phone rang. It was Claire. She sounded so happy. She said, "Mum, did you read Olivia's poem on Facebook? It's so beautiful." I said, "I haven't," and looked at Olivia curiously as she hadn't said a thing about it the whole day. I explained to Claire that Olivia was with me and so was Kathy and Maryanne and would she like to read the poem to us, which she did. We were blown away.

How beautiful that moment was that brought us all together. The bond was so powerful—all due to one brilliant blue bohemian butterfly that had touched our hearts forever.

It was a very sacred time. We were all displaced in one way or another and yet by having so much support it kept me going, sometimes at my own peril. I recall one evening that I woke up to what I thought was a very bad cramp. I found myself in agony, trying to relieve the symptoms. All I could think of was my brilliant blue bohemian butterfly and how so many times she must have been in pain and my heart felt a huge pang.

I realised that I was not succeeding in either consoling myself or improving my situation, so I went and wrapped a bandage around my foot and put a heat pack on it. I nestled back into my warm bed, trying hard to remain calm and let the heat and the bandage do its job.

As I was just starting to drift off I heard Anna singing to *Wild Wind* and knew immediately that it was the DVD playing in her room. It was a tribute to her life. How could it play without anyone pressing it to start? I lay there.

I decided not to freak out, which was my first reaction, and instead I decided to listen to the music and Anna's voice while my foot was throbbing. I realised that she wanted to get my attention. She was telling me that I needed to slow down and keep to my promise of looking after myself. Clearly she felt that I needed a reminder. When I limped the next day to the doctor he looked at my foot and said, "Susan, has someone grabbed you?" I smiled. I told him the story and he also smiled. He knew Anna and he knew our bond. I'm pleased to say that I have not had another experience like that since, however I listened and I have been mindful of my own needs and of my promise to Anna.

After the special visitors had returned to their homes, I felt in my heart that it was time to have some sacred time to myself. I had promised Anna that I would look after myself and that I would also continue to embrace the art of 'being' and to follow my passion.

In keeping with that promise, after the visitors left, it was time for me to head south toward northern New South Wales for my pilgrimage. I didn't know exactly how far south I would go but I knew I could trust my instincts when I had arrived at my mystery destination. After packing the car I headed through Fortitude Valley and drove across the Story Bridge. Nothing prepared me for the overwhelming sadness I felt as I drove past St Vincent's Private Hospital, Brisbane. I was still crying when I crossed the Queensland/New South Wales border an hour and a half later. The grief just poured out of me. It made me realise that I shouldn't drive too far and so I went off the highway when I saw a sign for Kingscliff.

As soon as I saw a white building with white shutters, nestled in the dunes and overlooking the blue ocean, I knew that was where I wanted to stay—I was drawn to it. The white and blue reminded me of Greece; for some reason I do not know even to this very day, during the period of Anna's full-time care, I started collecting paintings of Greece and putting them on my bedroom walls. They gave me hope. I kept imagining being there, relaxing in the Mediterranean and fulfilling my dreams.

So now I was able to enjoy this beautiful, serene place nestled in the sand dunes. I was only intending to stay a day or two before moving on, but I stayed five nights. I didn't go anywhere. I was in the most perfect sanctuary where my heart could grieve and I could have time to reflect. The room was perfect. It had a lounge with a wraparound deck and a kitchen bench that was the right height and shape for me to continue painting the canvases that Anna and I had been working on together. It was so therapeutic, finishing the piece.

Each day the cat's eyes, which represented Anna's nine lives, seemed brighter as the design unfolded. There were flowing lines that depicted the many twists and turns in Anna's life and the river meandering its way through the painting represented the joy it brought to her life. It had vibrant colours of yellow, blue, and green. I discretely wrote the names of her devoted team into the painting as they were integral to her happiness. Two sacred sunflowers represented her tribute and proudly displayed in the centre was a blue heart—half on each canvas. I named the painting *A Mother and Daughter's HeART*.

I didn't see many people during my pilgrimage but the ones I met were children, and a young traveller in a Kombi. They each touched my soul as their conversations somehow managed to send the same message—to live in the moment and to embrace life. It was reaffirming.

It was strange leaving on the sixth day. Each day I had simply gone and booked another night until I felt my pain had eased and that I was ready to return to the world.

When I now recollect my feelings of that week, from the first day when I felt so empty standing on the beach at Kingscliff, to when I got in the car to return home, it was all so profound. Through painting, walking, time out, reflecting, crying, and soul-searching, I started the healing process. I also started to feel an inner peace in the grief. It had been a pilgrimage.

Lesson 78: Take time out to reflect and just be

Upon returning home I remembered that there was an art exhibition being held in May at the Robina Community Centre at the Gold Coast—The Woman's heART Exhibition. It was part of the Women's Health and Wellbeing Expo.

I contacted them and was delighted that they accepted *A Mother and Daughter's heART* as part of their art exhibition. On the opening night Professor McConnell came with his wife and twin sons. My brother-in-law's cousin who I hadn't seen for years also came. She told me the amazing story of how she had been on a bus tour in Adelaide when she heard the news about Anna's passing. A fellow passenger was sitting behind her and said, "Oh that's sad, she was such a fighter," and Suzanne asked him more about who it was. He said, "She was a twenty-nine-year-old remarkable woman who beat all the odds who has just passed away. Her name was Anna." With that, Suzanne asked whether it was Anna

Paas. He replied that it was. She then decided to contact my brother-in-law, Bruce, upon her return home. He had told her that I would be in Robina for the opening, and as she lived nearby she had decided to be there to support me. I was very touched, just as I was by the fact that the professor and his family were there, too. There were over 100 people at the opening. Anna's painting hung proudly in the gallery and her story was told throughout the week of the exhibition. It was yet another tribute to Anna and her remarkable life.

Lesson 79: Trust in the ways things unfold—they are how they are meant to be

I felt it was important to also revisit places in Brisbane where Anna loved going along the river. On the day that the Sydney Street City Cat Terminal opened at the end of May, after being closed for reconstruction since January, I decided it was the right time to start my river journey.

The first stop was Riverside where I went to the café where Anna loved going. I ordered an omelette. It was very emotional and I could hardly eat it. The waitress wondered why Anna wasn't with me and this, I found, was the question that came up each time. What became apparent to me was that it had not been obvious that Anna was terminally ill. In fact, she was the happiest I had ever seen her during the last few months of her life. I coped reasonably well and got through the omelette and then walked to where Anna and I had our complimentary high tea last Christmas. I really didn't expect the manager to remember me or that he would even be there. However, when I walked into the restaurant, there he was. He smiled and asked, "Where is your gorgeous daughter?" This time I didn't keep my composure. I literally started sobbing. He got me a glass of water and left me to compose myself. He returned, explaining that he needed to leave as he was very distressed. The strange thing was that he'd only met Anna and me once before. He told me how much of an impression we had made. He could not let us just walk away—he had been touched by our bond and he wanted to offer us a treat.

I told him that's why I had come back to see him. I wanted to thank him for giving me such special memories of Anna's last Christmas where he had been so generous and that I would cherish forever a video taken of us both sitting at the table with the white linen tablecloth and our coffees (with extra froth!) and our high tea. We were so happy. He had given us a precious gift that I would cherish forever.

That day I also bought a special ring, which I had not intended to buy. I was walking past a jeweller when I saw the Mother's Day sign in the shape of a heart. I sobbed my heart out and the ladies in the shop sat me down and brought me some water. I explained why I was so upset. They were very understanding. There in front of me was a beautiful ring. It was a London blue topaz with diamonds and white gold. I asked if I could try it on. It fitted perfectly. I also explained that I hadn't come in to buy a ring but to replace two bed pillows, which I was hanging on to under each arm as though I had air-cushions under me for support, which as it turned out I needed. They phoned Head Office and came back with a deal I couldn't refuse. Now I had two new pillows and a ring.

I tucked it safely in my bag and then made a decision that on Mother's Day I would open it with Claire via Skype. It made Mother's Day special. Claire and I enjoyed the moment when she saw the ring come out of the case, and the beautiful London blue topaz gem, which reminded me of Claire (being in the UK) and Anna because it was sky blue. The diamonds meant they were both with me forever. It was an important moment when Claire and I bonded even more closely as we had performed a ritual that represented the start of our new paths as mother and daughter with Anna by our side as our guardian angel.

Lesson 80: Be generous, kind, and empathetic

On 29 May 2015 I attended the Thanksgiving Service at St John's Cathedral in Ann Street in Brisbane to celebrate National Palliative Care Week.

Throughout the service, I felt myself reflecting on Anna's life and on how it was a life well-lived. I also recognised that Anna, particularly as she neared the end of her life, let me see the depths of her soul. I recognised the importance of honouring a loved one's wishes from birth to death. Our time we shared together was sacred. It will be in my heart and spirit forever. It has enabled me to feel truly authentic. My eyes now see through different lenses. They have been fine-tuned and have given me clarity for my higher purpose.

I am so grateful to my brilliant blue bohemian butterfly for the treasure that she left of eighty-five universal life lessons from the tapestry of her life, now revealed lovingly on the pages of this book through the colourful and heartfelt stories from when she was born in 1985.

Lesson 81: Let your higher purpose shine through

Chapter 10
Reflecting

It is with heartfelt pride that I share with you, in the last chapter of the book, the eulogies that were lovingly read at Anna's Sacred Sunflower Service, which was held at the Merthyr Uniting Church on 22 April 2015. It shows how Anna touched the hearts of many and left the world a better place.

Lesson 82: Leave your legacy and make the world a better place

ANNA'S EULOGY
By Susan

Anna, I can just imagine you today looking down at us in our colours of blue, checking out the fashion and making sure we are organised and accessorised. I also suspect you are on the case already in your new place where I can imagine you with brightly coloured wings and a cheeky smile, making sure everything is in order. They won't know what's hit them. It certainly is their gain.

What an amazing journey you had here in this life, Anna. You surprised everyone with your stamina, willpower, determination, sense of humour, and amazing strength of character—beating all the odds and just being downright loveable and adorable. You had qualities, Anna, that I must admit were truly exceptional. You had gifts that many people never acquire in a lifetime—you had them in abundance.

When leaving the hospital after you had passed away, the head nurse commented that I had had a little girl who never went through the teen years and who never worried about adulthood. I hadn't thought about it like that before, but it was true—Anna was pure and gave unconditional love in bucket-loads and never had to worry about life's trials and tribulations. However, she also had a life that gave her more than her fair share of challenges and yet she was always happy and was never put off by what was thrown at her.

I'd like to share some of her amazing story with you ... Anna Rose Paas was born on 18 October 1985. She was born at Boothville Hospital in Windsor, Brisbane, where her sister Claire had been born and where I had been born somewhat earlier!

I was aware of Anna's special qualities from a very early age. As a baby, Anna slept a lot, particularly from birth into her first year. I remember Anna having floppy muscles and, as a result, I often carried her over my arm from six months—just like carrying a sack of potatoes (sorry Anna)!

Throughout the early months and years Anna avoided eye contact. She also found it difficult to show when she was hungry, hot, cold, sick, or in pain.

One month prior to Anna's second birthday, she was diagnosed with Ring Chromosome 22 and following the diagnosis Anna was referred to a genetic counsellor. At this time very little hope was given to Anna—they said she would not walk or talk and would be a vegetable. Anna, at this time, was not acknowledging us and she was living very much in her own personal 'inner world'. Who would have thought then that Anna would live to twenty-nine years of age, which was far beyond her life expectancy.

A significant turning point in Anna's life was when our family; Michael (Anna's Dad), Claire, and I moved to Victoria and Anna was referred to a specialist who was the co-ordinator of the Early Intervention Program in Geelong, Victoria. Anna undertook a rigorous three-year program including occupational therapy, physiotherapy, crawling, and trampolining—which Anna continued for many years and became very proficient at, until one day, in true Anna style, she decided that she didn't want to go on the trampoline anymore. So that was that.

Through this early intervention, Anna continued to improve and she also started to use Makaton sign language, which made her less frustrated. She successfully finished the program and our family returned to Brisbane in 1990. We also made a decision not to think about Anna having Ring 22 but focused on Anna being extended to her fullest potential and giving her the wings to fly.

In June 1991 two students from QUT undertook a study, 'Observations of an Exceptional Child in an Early Childhood Classroom/Home Setting'. The exceptional child was Anna. I would love to share some observations from when they visited Anna at home and at the Kelvin Grove Childcare Centre, to show how far she came from those early years.

> Anna showed me around her home by holding my hand and pulling me to follow her. She took particular attention showing me her older sister's room and her own room. We stopped for a while and played with her two kittens. She crouched down to their level, pointing, vocalising, and showing a face full of expression. Anna then showed me her rocking horse and I lifted her on and she was so happy rocking on it. She then showed me her Peter Rabbit toy and then took me by the hand to her sister's room to show me the dolls' house. When it was time for me to go, Anna walked me outside. Anna held my hand down the stairs and to the front gate and waved and said 'bye' as I left.

Another was a visit to the centre. On this occasion they chose to view Anna as part of the group and to actively watch and share in Anna's afternoon.

> Anna showed much delight in the extra attention and was excited throughout our visit. Anna noticed musical instruments and invited us to play by handing instruments

to us—she danced, skipped and shook the maracas. Another child took off her dancing costume and offered it to Anna. Anna said 'yep' and the other child helped to put the dress on Anna with a small amount of teacher assistance. We certainly found a very secure, independent and confident child who was very much part of the childcare setting.

With this progress, Anna commenced at Mitchelton Special School where she continued developing her independence. She loved it when the school bus came to our home in Ashgrove to pick her up in the morning. She also loved it when she went to Lyn and Trevor's in the afternoon after school. They were just wonderful to Anna and were wonderful neighbours.

There were also some interesting developments happening in our family, too, and during this time I met Colin and he embraced both Anna and Claire. It wasn't long before we were all packing up and heading off to England to live in a little village in West Sussex called Cuckfield.

Anna enrolled in Court Meadow Special School where she soon had many friends and a Link Mum, Sally, who loved having Anna when I was away in London. Sally has remained very close to Anna and our family and came to Australia to see her several years ago and recently posted her a very huggable bear.

It was fun to watch Anna become more and more confident and get involved in musical productions. She even sang at our wedding in England in 2002 with Shine, a group of delightful young people. And shine they certainly did. When they would sing 'Something Inside So Strong' Anna came alive, making signs and singing with so much gusto and absolute joy. It was wonderful to watch. We have a DVD to show how proud she was when she was singing with Shine, and her absolute sheer joy when singing at our wedding. I can't remember how many pizzas were devoured over the six weeks of rehearsals with the girls on Sundays, but it sure was fun and Anna had an absolute ball.

She also brought tears to the eyes of the locals in Cuckfield on the eve of our departure when we put on a farewell event at The White Harte where everyone had to come dressed as Aussies. At the end of the night many people made farewell speeches (looking rather funny with their Aussie gear and whiteout on their noses!). Unexpectedly when someone sang out, "Does anyone else want to make a speech?" Anna put her hand up and confidently spoke for ten minutes in her own lingo. There wasn't a dry eye in the house. I was so proud of Anna and I told her so as we were walking through the churchyard on our way home from the pub. She was just glowing with pride.

Anna also made an impact at Colin's valedictory dinner where he was making a formal speech to a packed auditorium. As he commenced and said, "Your Excellencies, Ladies and Gentleman," Anna loudly said 'yes' and the audience murmured, wondering who it was. Colin smiled and simply said, "And, yes, sorry ...

and Anna." He proudly stated that Anna was his stepdaughter. After the formalities everyone wanted to meet Anna!

She was also a star at our wedding when Colin was having trouble putting the ring on my finger. Anna very excitedly said, "Get it on, Colin," and we were both stunned at her tenacity that day. She later confidently said, "Come on, Claire, hurry up," and led Claire out of the registry office downstairs to the procession.

Jake's Dad recalls: "Anna was a lovely soul. It is one of my favourite past memories watching Shark Tale and the Little Mermaid, when Anna was living in the UK. I will never forget her sheer joy at getting to watch it with her sister and Jake."

During this time, too, we visited Italy regularly. Anna was so embraced by the Italians. Her favourite pastime there was having gelatos. She would simply just point to the gelato she wanted and say, "Prego!" (This worked a treat.) She just kept pointing to different ones and they never seemed to care how many she had. The more she had, the happier they were.

We then returned to Brisbane, when Anna was nineteen, as it was an important time for her to transition from school into the next phase of her life. She was a great swimmer and Colin would tell her to 'kick, Anna' and in the end she would save him from saying it as she would say out loud (sometimes gurgling with water in her mouth), "Good girl—kick, Anna, kick." She also loved going to TAFE and the horticulture and hospitality courses.

Anna had a wicked sense of humour. Once, at a family gathering, when her father and her uncle were in the same room and looking every bit identical twins with their grey beards, she was dressed and ready for bed and was walking around saying goodnight to everyone. "Goodnight," she said, and leaned forward for a kiss. "Goodnight Dad," she said to John, her uncle. Anna's Dad Michael sat up and said, "Well, who am I then?" Quite as a flash, Anna retorted, "Santa." It was just such funny and quite sophisticated humour. That was Anna.

At twenty, Anna became very ill when it was discovered that she had an inoperable brain tumour and health problems reoccurred. By twenty-one, Anna was living in supported accommodation at Mercy Community Services at Wooloowin and during the next eight years, when Anna was in and out of hospital with serious neurological conditions, Mercy was just brilliant, enabling her to transition back into her home. Anna spent many Christmases in hospital. Somehow Anna had a body clock that said every November/December, it was time to get sick! Fortunately the last two years she was home for Christmas, thank goodness! Obviously her body clock was told to behave!

To show Anna's strength of character in 2013 she received a beautiful birthday card from Kate from Mercy, which read:

> Inspiring, amazing, strong, beautiful, courageous, fighter, and magnetic. These are just a few of the words that come to mind when we think of you. You never give

up and you make the world a better place just by being the wonderful person you are. Thank you for being such an inspiration and for showing that no matter what, it is better to fight for what you want, rather than stay silent. That is a rare trait to have and you do it perfectly. Happy birthday Anna.

Since the age of twenty-seven, Anna had her own car and loved being able to go out and about with Kathy, Olivia, Amy, and Beth. Often they would go to art classes at Access Arts, where Anna just loved being an artist and showcasing her artistic gifts and talents. In preparation for the G20, she attended sewing classes where they made their outfits to wear in the G20 parade.

I recall very fondly that when we got dressed, Pat, our dear friend, came with all the gear and put some of the accessories on the dining room table for Anna, Olivia, Pat, and me to choose from so that we could add to our ensembles.

Anna went to the table and saw the belly dancer skirt and said 'nice' and added that to her outfit, she saw a red sash—'nice'—and she added that to her outfit. In fact, everything that was on the table she added to her outfit and she looked an absolute treat.

The highlight wasn't the G20 parade, it was walking from the City Cat stop at QUT to the meeting point. It was like *The Sound of Music* as Anna held hands between Pat and me and sang all her favourite tunes; 'Frere Jacques', 'If You're Happy and You Know It', 'Oranges and Lemons'.

It was as though Anna had come alive and that day last November, she was at her most glorious. What a vivid memory I have etched in my heart of that day. It was just so precious.

During this time, Anna also made a decision that she would not have any more medical intervention and she and I worked together with Professor Harry McConnell and his team at the Health Advocacy Legal Clinic (HALC) at St Vincent's Private Hospital, Brisbane, to prepare her Statement of Views, better known as an Advance Care Plan, ensuring her wishes for quality of life.

I am very proud to say that her wishes were honoured and that it enabled Anna to make choices with her taking control of those decisions. In fact, Anna, I am so proud of you and how you lived your life. You were so brave and courageous. You taught us so much and the learning I have taken is to truly treasure the precious moments and memories I have of you. I am so grateful that I have many. You brought so much joy to my life and to so many. I absolutely loved being your mum and I will love you for eternity. I have watched the devotion of your team who have been by your side. They have shone in your time of need and I am eternally grateful for their love and commitment to you.

Colin, you were also so devoted to Anna and your love for her shone through always and Anna knew she was dearly loved. Anna—I will always have you close to my heart and hold that memory of the twinkle in your eye and your cheeky smile and that cute giggle—you are now my guardian angel forever.

ANNA'S EULOGY
By Sally, Anna's Link Mum

It was hard at first, really hard, to think of someone as beautiful as Anna passing—but then, as day slowly turned into night, that sadness was replaced by happy thoughts of all the wonderful times we shared together on my journey as Anna's Link Family. I've supported a lot of youngsters with special needs over the years, and each time the parents have been quick to point out just how much it means, both to them and to their children, to have the support of people like me.

I'm always touched by their words of gratitude. But what those parents must also remember is that I, too, get so much out of the time that I spend with their children. And in fact, the lessons I have learned from those children over the years—lessons in unconditional love and acceptance—are potentially far more important than anything more tangible that I have to offer them.

Anna always had an amazing little twinkle in her eye and was ready to take on absolutely anything, with confidence and a spirit of utter determination that you couldn't help but admire. It didn't matter what happened, whatever obstacle life threw in her way, Anna had a way of hitting back with a renewed sense of resolve that many of us would struggle to find. What more inspiration could you need than someone as beautiful as Anna?

I remember sitting down to the dinner table on countless occasions with a teenaged Anna, trying to encourage her to chew her food first before swallowing.

She'd look at me and, through a mouthful of dinner, say 'chew', demonstrating that she knew exactly what was expected of her, before gulping down the whole, untouched mouthful in one go!

Back then, Anna loved trampolining. If ever she came to stay with me on a Monday, I'd take her along to trampolining sessions with many of her school friends, where she'd amuse the instructor, Jane, with a string of cross-legged 'seat drops', one after the other, regardless of what she was actually being asked to do at the time! It was a delight to watch.

There were times when Anna would call down the stairs to me—"Saaaaaaalllllyyyyyy!"—and I'd go to the bottom of the stairs, reply with a "Yes, Anna?" and she'd look at me with a totally bemused expression and say, "What?" This used to have the pair of us in hysterics—I don't think I ever did find out what she wanted! And she was very quick to dish out instructions in her own absolutely unique but incredibly endearing lingo, and then finish up with one hand on her hip, a stern glare, and a firm, "Ok?" Yup, got it! Won't do that again, Anna!

I learnt very quickly that it wasn't wise to say anything to Anna that could be interpreted too literally. As you or I might do to our friends, I once asked her to 'just chuck that over here'. I had to duck as the required item sailed through the air, dangerously close to my head.

And as anyone with kids knows, they don't often like to wait until the adult is up and about before starting their day. Anna was no exception. You know how it is; you wake up, bleary-eyed, when it's still dark outside, disturbed by what could have been a noise coming from the kid's bedroom next door. Listening out for a moment, but hearing nothing further, you roll over and pull the pillow over your head, content that the child must actually still be fast asleep. Half an hour later, you wake again, convinced you aren't yet losing the plot and that you probably did hear something the first time after all. And then you venture sheepishly into the child's bedroom, wondering what horrors you might find there.

On that particular occasion, I had heard the word 'writing' spoken aloud. Of course, at 6am I had thought nothing of it, but then, going into Anna's room, there she was, sat bolt upright in bed, with my writing paper and a packet of envelopes spread out in front of her. Having written her name on the corner of every single piece of paper and envelope in the folder, her hand was poised ready to write her name on my wall! As I took in the (rather amusing) scene before me, Anna just grinned and said simply, "What?"

Susan has already mentioned just how independent Anna liked to be. I'll never forget Susan telling me about the morning Anna got out of bed in Cuckfield and decided to make her own breakfast. Susan remained blissfully unaware of this incident, until such a point as the smell of fiercely burning toast drifted up the stairs …

She's mentioned, too, Anna's rendition of 'Something Inside So Strong'. That song is the very first thing that came to mind when I heard the sad news. It's one of my favourite memories of Anna; everything about that performance showed her true character shining through and, if we could pick a song that defined us, that's the one I'd choose for Anna. She really did have 'something inside so strong'—encouraged, in no small part, by her wonderful family, and in particular her amazing mother Susan.

When they moved back to Australia, I didn't see Anna for a number of years but always kept in touch, always heard how she was getting on back in Brisbane. And when I finally found the time and money to venture over there, I was taken straight round to Anna's house to surprise her. Susan hadn't told her that I was coming. On seeing me knocking at the door, Anna's jaw dropped slightly and then, without a word, she simply took my hand, led me to the sofa, and invited me to sit next to her to watch her *Playschool* DVD with her. I knew then that even though I'd not seen her in person in years, Anna hadn't forgotten me.

And Anna, I will never forget you. You will always have a special place in my heart and I know you'll be here, in your own unique and special way, looking out for us all.

ANNA'S EULOGY
By Colin

In the language of today, Anna would be described as 'special needs'. That's not right. Anna was just *special*. She was special in many ways. Rather than dwell on those that have been described by others, I want to mention just a few of her special skills and qualities, ones that illustrate other aspects—some of them humorous, I hope—of just how special she was.

First, she had the special skills and qualities required of the diplomat; something I know a lot about. Susan has already told the story about when she called her uncle 'Santa'. I take this as a sign of great diplomatic skill on Anna's part!

On the other hand, there were Anna's equally outstanding skills of what can best be described as 'non-diplomacy'. During our years in England, we came back on leave after three or four of those years. When we checked in at Heathrow to begin the long journey home we were, at first, given three seats in different places in business class and only after much argy-bargy were we given three seats together. But when we boarded the plane (among the last to do so) we were told that a mistake had been made and that we had to have the original three seats. We refused. The reasons were understood and the chief cabin services man went back into the plane.

A full half-an-hour passed before he returned, flustered no doubt from having to persuade many on board to move to other seats. Eventually we boarded, and found an atmosphere of anger and disdain, having long-delayed the flight's departure. As we went up the aisle to take our seats, Anna swung her small backpack off her shoulders, not realising that immediately behind her a stewardess was serving, from a large tray, glasses of champagne to calm the angry passengers. The effect was dramatic: those behind, even those several rows back, were showered with the very bubbly champagne!

I think it was at the end of the same journey that Anna displayed—not for the first time, I might add—her astounding memory. We had not been home for at least three years. We took a taxi from the airport to our home, which was then in Ashgrove. Long before we reached it, she was telling the driver with great accuracy 'left here', 'right here', 'straight on' and so on. All those years on, she had remembered!

And then there was Anna the socialite. After every party or gathering of family or friends, Anna would say goodbye in her own inimitable style. This meant going up to one person and asking Susan or me, "This one now?" and then hugging or shaking hands—she would then go to the next person— "This one now?" and so on until the last.

My final recollection of Anna's special skills is of when we left England after our seven years there when Anna made her speech of a lifetime. Anna the orator ... who would have guessed it?

Finally, although this is about Anna, I want to say a few words about her mother. Simply this: Susan has been, for twenty-nine years, more loving of and devoted to her daughter than could be imagined. She has, on Anna's behalf, fought, lobbied, advocated, defended, attacked, and demanded, often all at once. She deserves respect, admiration, and love for what she has done.

Thank you Susan, for it is you who enabled Anna to be the remarkable person that she was.

ANNA'S EULOGY
By Bruce, Susan's brother-in-law

In the game of life Anna was not dealt a good hand. Hearts—she could love and she certainly was loved by all who knew her. She also got the Joker, she loved to laugh and enjoy a joke. Most of all she had an Ace and that was her mother.

Susan cared for Anna unstintingly and completely for her entire life.

As we come here to celebrate Anna's life, so short and so amazingly challenging, we can all think of many occasions when she touched our hearts.

Let's also think of Susan as she begins a very different life. Her dedication to her daughter and the life that she gave her is a triumph of love over adversity.

Now, as she adjusts to a new life, I know that everyone here today is committed to giving her the love and support that she needs at this time.

Vale Anna Rose Paas, we thank you for the joy that you brought to us all.

ANNA'S EULOGY
Read by Barbara on behalf of Michael, Claire, and Jake

I am Barbara Snook, a long-time family friend, and I would like to bring you some words from Anna's Dad, Michael, and his wife, Paula, who were not able to be at the service today. Michael asked that I share his words with you.

> Anna has been fortunate to have Susan and Colin at her side on the many occasions that she needed them. Her smile always shone through in gratitude.

Thank you Michael. Jake, too, wanted to say what he remembered about his Aunty Anna ...

> I'd like to say a few words about how special my Aunty Anna was to me. When I was young she was here in the UK with Nanna and Colin, so I saw her quite a bit. One of the times I remember in particular was when Mum was giving me an excessive amount of attention once when Anna was staying with us. This didn't impress Anna at all who then proceeded to pretend she was sick, doing a bad fake cough and pointing at her throat, saying, "Ow!" Anna then lay in my bed and asked my mum for 'tea peease!'. I think Anna was used to getting it quite good with my Nanna! When I got a bit older Anna made me laugh by blaming me if anyone was naughty (including herself on many, many occasions!). She would quickly call 'Ja-ake' and point at me! She always made me laugh. My Aunty Anna, you'll always have a place in my heart. We miss you xx

Thank you Jake—it was lovely hearing about your special memories of your beloved aunty.

I would now like to share some special words from Claire, who is Anna's sister and lives in Brighton, England, with her son Jake and daughter Mia. She is unable to be with us today but has been reflecting on Anna's life and her relationship with her sister through emails to her mother. Susan has asked that these thoughts are shared here with all of you here present.

> I have no idea how to describe how I'm feeling, nor, I am sure, do you. I just watched a Skype video of you with Anna from only the beginning of this month. You were the best person and mother in the whole world EVER to Anna—make sure you know that! And to me too of course but I can still tell you that. I need to speak for Anna as well. Thank you for being there, always, for us. I'm letting myself be a bit sad as I have a few hours to myself and that's how I feel; I miss you my beautiful baby sister.
>
> I remember you being pregnant forever with Anna in your tummy and people always asked me when you were due. I only remember you being pregnant and looking like a hippo because I was asked so often when you were having the baby, and I thought 'never!'. When Anna finally came, she made herself very known and never stopped giving us all the love she had to give; it seemed like more than most people ever have, let alone give. I'll always have my sister. I'll always hear her saying, "Come on Claire!" telling me to hurry up—she was always right too, and so brave and happy with the life she had—and she had so much. Anna loved us all so very much, just completely without ever growing up and having the problems of life burden her and weigh her down. She just got to love us and that was due to you. We have so many good memories to hold close.
>
> Growing up we played thousands of games of *Monopoly* at Bonma's place and one time Anna drew all over the board with crayon. I couldn't

get it off—but I tried. I just keep thinking of all the nice times we shared. Funny times, hard times, nice times.

I was looking at photos of her swimming years ago. She was strong, able, and tried so hard. You couldn't have made life better for her. She was lucky it was you she was born to, her life could have been so different had she been born to someone else. We were all lucky.

Without you

Each day passes now
Without you darling girl
So many thoughts I'm holding tight
Of your laughter, saying 'Claire' with all your might
I watched as you grew
Surpassed all who thought they knew about you
Blossoming as you entwined our hearts
Fighting to become the beautiful, kind girl
With a soul so deep, who we're all so pleased we knew
We couldn't have asked you to do more
The strength, it was all you my sweet
The love you had for life, complete
We've learnt from you, darling Anna
To love all we have, for the time we are able
For you precious girl, you've finally had to let go
'Hold hands Claire', you'd say to me
Darling, I'm not letting go xxxxxxxx

Thank you Claire.

I am sure that many of us here relate to Claire's words. Claire was not too many years older than Anna, and, as a young girl, she spent time supporting her Mum in minding Anna when Anna was young. While everyone here would agree with Claire's words that acknowledge Susan as an amazing mother, we must also thank you, Claire, for your part as a beautiful and loving sister.

> *Lesson 83: Celebrate a loved one's life by expressing your thoughts and feelings*

It seems so right that *Universal Life Lessons from My Brilliant Blue Bohemian Butterfly* should finish with the words from Claire, a very special young woman who, being Anna's sister, has now the right of passage to take her new position in the family where her sister lives with her in her heart and soul as her guardian angel—as she is mine.

> *Lesson 84: Recognise that every person has their rightful place and role to play*

Through my weaving the stories of Anna's life together through the fabric of this book, I hope you have enjoyed stepping into our world and learning about the eighty-five universal life lessons, some of which are specific to Anna and others that are more general ideas of entering community, focusing on qualities and gifts, taking control of your own decisions, and embracing difference.

My brilliant blue bohemian butterfly would be, I'm sure, thrilled to know that her story has been told to give hope to others and make a difference to the world.

Lesson 85: Make a difference to the world

Learnings
Universal Life Lessons

Lesson 1: Be grateful for small steps and celebrate them with all your heart

Lesson 2: Reach out to the people you need on your journey

Lesson 3: Trust in unexpected moments that bring hope and joy

Lesson 4: Person-centred storybooks are valuable tools and enablers

Lesson 5: Strengthening core muscles at an early age is very important

Lesson 6: Make learning fun and engaging

Lesson 7: An early intervention program is beneficial for development and wellness

Lesson 8: Anger and aggressive behaviour might be frustration—signing can assist

Lesson 9: See the person, not the disability

Lesson 10: Inclusion at an early age, and with support, is extremely important

Lesson 11: Capture the evidence of your child's development

Lesson 12: Provide the tools throughout a child's journey to enable growth and development
Lesson 13: Accept, include, and value each person and celebrate their differences
Lesson 14: Embrace exceptionality and uniqueness, we are all the same but different
Lesson 15: Inner joy and connecting in heart space is contagious—spread the love
Lesson 16: Encourage laughter and a sense of humour
Lesson 17: Be mindful of others—let them shine
Lesson 18: Due diligence and trusting in your decisions gives you strength
Lesson 19: Encourage independence, communication, and confidence
Lesson 20: Acknowledge and encourage siblings to be supportive of one another
Lesson 21: Provide routine and consistency
Lesson 22: Autistic tendencies can be reduced by stimulation and encouragement
Lesson 23: Respect others' likes and dislikes
Lesson 24: Swimming enhances wellness, circulation, and fitness
Lesson 25: A stimulating environment increases learning and developmental potential
Lesson 26: Singing promotes creativity and ignites passion and joy
Lesson 27: Embracing your local community enhances your quality of life
Lesson 28: Share precious moments with others to bring them on your journey

Lesson 29: Take risks—expect the unexpected and let the different worlds entwine
Lesson 30: Know your rights and never give up
Lesson 31: Calm advocacy and innovative solutions encourage the best outcome
Lesson 32: Believe in others and they will rise to it
Lesson 33: Communicating from the heart is authentic
Lesson 34: Enjoy the journey, not just the destination
Lesson 35: We are role models and our actions are observed by others
Lesson 36: Sometimes gifts come in the most unexpected ways—treasure them
Lesson 37: Enjoy the simple things and small pleasures of life
Lesson 38: Take pride in your community—participate and be engaged
Lesson 39: Always believe in knights in shining armour
Lesson 40: Be generous of spirit—give gifts that touch people's lives
Lesson 41: Be brave—deviate and develop new plans, then embrace them
Lesson 42: Connecting communities enriches lives
Lesson 43: Circumstances may change but it is the precious moments that count
Lesson 44: Acknowledge and celebrate strengths and build on them
Lesson 45: Be mindful of precious moments that then become poignant memories
Lesson 46: Be adaptive, responsive, and prepared to change how you do things

Lesson 47: Keep fit and healthy—enjoy the outdoor life whenever you can
Lesson 48: If you are an artist, leave a legacy of your beautiful creations
Lesson 49: Capture and share the important lessons of your life
Lesson 50: Trust that the right people are on your journey
Lesson 51: Value friendships and what they bring to your life
Lesson 52: Awaken your spirituality by trusting in synchronicity
Lesson 53: Embrace sacred time with your family and friends
Lesson 54: Don't accept the status quo—defend your loved one's rights
Lesson 55: Provide a safe, familiar environment and nurture a sense of belonging
Lesson 56: Mentor others in the art of being person-centred
Lesson 57: Invite others into your world which builds awareness and empathy
Lesson 58: Be the custodian of knowledge for your loved ones
Lesson 59: Focus on the person, not on the medical condition
Lesson 60: Art can inspire renewed hope, rejuvenation, and reconnection
Lesson 61: Give it a go—even if it fails, it provides insight and valuable lessons

UNIVERSAL LIFE LESSONS

Lesson 62: Ring a friend when you need help
Lesson 63: Source specialists who understand your condition
Lesson 64: Break the rules—do whatever it takes to improve the situation
Lesson 65: Live in the present, celebrate the now
Lesson 66: Appreciate that tough times can make the good times seem so much better
Lesson 67: Prepare for end of life by honouring your loved one's wishes with integrity
Lesson 68: Surroundings that are welcoming and safe provide peace and comfort
Lesson 69: Practise random acts of kindness, they bring joy and happiness
Lesson 70: Take control of your health with regular check-ups and natural therapies
Lesson 71: Allow yourself to be vulnerable
Lesson 72: Clarify the person's wishes and give them control
Lesson 73: When you show your vulnerability, you let others in
Lesson 74: Rejoice in the unexpected pleasures of life
Lesson 75: Be daring and resourceful and take control of the situation
Lesson 76: Celebrate life to the end
Lesson 77: A fitting tribute to celebrate a loved one's life helps with grieving
Lesson 78: Take time out to reflect and just be
Lesson 79: Trust in the ways things unfold—they are how they are meant to be

Lesson 80: Be generous, kind, and empathetic
Lesson 81: Let your higher purpose shine through
Lesson 82: Leave your legacy and make the world a better place
Lesson 83: Celebrate a loved one's life by expressing your thoughts and feelings
Lesson 84: Recognise that every person has their rightful place and role to play
Lesson 85: Make a difference to the world

Glossary

A **Geneticist** is a person who studies or specialises in genetics, which is the study of heredity, or how the characteristics of living things are transmitted from one generation to the next. Every living thing contains the genetic material that makes up DNA molecules. This material is passed on when organisms reproduce.

An **Ophthalmologist** is a physician (doctor of medicine, MD, or doctor of osteopathy, DO) who specialises in the medical and surgical care of the eyes and visual system and in the prevention of eye disease and injury.

Occupational Therapy is a client-centred health profession concerned with promoting health and wellbeing through occupation. The primary goal of occupational therapy is to enable people to participate in the activities of everyday life. Occupational therapists achieve this outcome by working with people and communities to enhance their ability to engage in the occupations they want to, need to, or are expected to do, or by modifying the occupation or the environment to better support their occupational engagement.

Physiotherapy is a healthcare profession that assesses, diagnoses, treats, and works to prevent disease and disability through physical means. Physiotherapists are experts in movement and function who work in partnership with their patients, assisting them to overcome movement disorders, which may have been present from birth, acquired through accident or injury, or are the result of ageing or life-changing events.

Social Work is a professional and academic discipline that seeks to improve the quality of life and subjective wellbeing of individuals, families, couples, groups, and communities through research, policy, community organising, direct practice, crisis intervention, and teaching for the benefit of those affected by social disadvantages such as poverty, mental and physical illness or disability, and social injustice, including violations of their civil liberties and human rights. The profession is dedicated to the pursuit of social justice and the well-being of oppressed and marginalised individuals and communities. The social work profession is broad.

An **Individual Goals Plan** or **Personal Learning Plan** is developed by students, typically in collaboration with teachers, counsellors, and parents and as a way to help them achieve short- and long-term learning goals, most commonly at the middle school and high school levels.

A **Neurologist** is a doctor who specialises in treating diseases of the nervous system. The nervous system comprises the central and peripheral nervous system. This complex system involves the spinal cord and the brain.

A **Neurosurgeon** is a medical doctor or doctor of medicine who has completed a five- or six-year residency that focuses on the surgical treatment of patients with neurological conditions.

A **Neuropsychiatrist** is a medical specialist who deals with mental disorders attributable to diseases of the nervous system.

A **Gastroenterologist** is a physician who specialises in the diagnosis and treatment of diseases of the digestive system.

Hydrocephalus is a condition in which fluid accumulates in the brain, typically in young children, enlarging the head and sometimes causing brain damage.

A **Medical Shunt** is a hole or a small passage which moves, or allows movement of, fluid from one part of the body to another.

Advance Care Planning or preparation of a **Statement of Views** is a process of communication between individuals and their healthcare agents to understand, reflect on, discuss, and plan for future healthcare decisions for a time when individuals are not able to make their own healthcare decisions.

Resources

Makaton uses signs and symbols to help people communicate. www.makaton.org

Pyramid Educational Consultants (PECS) Australia offers training, consultation, and products that focus on teaching functional communication and designing effective educational environments across Australia, New Zealand, and South East Asia. They present a unique blend of broad-spectrum applied behaviour analysis and the development of functional communication skills, emphasising the individual needs of each person. www.pecsaustralia.com

PECS Images are teaching aids for people with learning difficulties. www.pecsimages.com

Rare Chromosome Disorder Support Group is to inform, support, and alleviate the isolation of anyone affected by a rare chromosome disorder and to raise public awareness. www.rarechromo.org

Chromosome 22 Central is a support group for families and individuals with disorders of chromosome 22. www.c22c.org www.facebook.com/pages/Chromosome-22-Central/170622056330115?ref=profile

Chromosome 22 Ring is a rare disorder characterized by abnormalities of the 22nd chromosome. wwwring22.org

Velocardiofacial Syndrome 22q11 Foundation is a not-for-profit support and awareness group. www.vcfs22q.org.au www.facebook.com/vcfs22q11?ref=profile

Angels with Missing Pieces 22q is a non-profit group for 22q11.2 deletion syndrome in the Kansas City area. www.amp22q.org www.facebook.com/amp22q?ref=profile

The Specials www.facebook.com/groups/TheSpecialsTVShow/?fref=ts www.facebook.com/TheSpecialsTVShow?fref=ts

Kangaroos is a charity providing leisure activities for disabled children and young adults in mid-Sussex. www.kangaroos.org.uk

West Sussex County Council offers support for adults with learning disabilities through their Community Learning Disability Team. www.westsussex.gov.uk/social-care-and-health/how-to-get-social-care-help/support-for-adults-with-learning-disabilities

St Vincent's Private Hospital, Brisbane is a not-for-profit hospital specialising in medical care for people with chronic and complex care needs. Through St Vincent's Private Hospital you can also contact the Health Advocacy Legal Clinic (HALC). www.svphb.org.au

Queensland Pain Clinic doctors are registered specialist pain medicine physicians and are experts in the management of all types of pain. Many people treated will be able to have their pain relieved by the use of medications or specialist procedures.

Some people unfortunately will have pain that is impossible to fully relieve; but can be helped to manage their lives in a way to minimise the effects of their pain with help from the clinic's specialists. www.qldpainclinic.com.au

Royal Brisbane and Women's Hospital (RBWH) is a 929-bed quaternary and tertiary referral teaching hospital located at the Herston site within Metro North Hospital and Health Service, close to the Brisbane CBD. www.health.qld.gov.au/rbwh

Blue Care has been providing care in Australia for over sixty years supporting the elderly, people with a disability, and others in their time of need. www.bluecare.org.au

Queensland Public Interest Law Clearing House (QPILCH) is a not-for-profit, community-based legal organisation that co-ordinates the provision of pro-bono legal services for individuals and community groups. www.qpilch.org.au

Access Arts Incorporated is a non-profit organisation assisting people with a disability or disadvantage to pursue their artistic ambitions. www.accessarts.org.au

Mercy Community Services is a values-based, boutique service organisation supporting people with an intellectual disability to pursue opportunities, develop and learn throughout their lives. We believe that each person is an individual who has spiritual, emotional, psychological, physical and social needs. We uphold the right of each individual to maintain their dignity, self-worth and respect. Each individual has a right to experience the fullness of what life has to offer, the right to make choices and be responsible for their decisions. www.disability.mercycs.org.au

Paint Your Life is a charity organisation working with very talented and professional artists to enhance the lives of disadvantaged and disabled people. www.paintyourlife.net.au

The Rotary Club of New Farm is a dynamic group of ordinary people working together to make the world a better place, starting with our own community. Rotary is a non-political, non-religious organisation open to every race, culture, and creed. www.rotarynewfarm.com

Universal Life Lessons provides an opportunity for you to connect with the author through her website. Susan is a global leader presenting Universal Life Lessons Workshops around the world. She is a public speaker and an Art of Hosting facilitator. Susan is also able to provide individual information, advice, and guidance sessions. *Universal Life Lessons from My Brilliant Blue Bohemian Butterfly* can be ordered through her website or via amazon as an eBook. www.universallifelessons.com

Afterword
Life Spirit

I first met my dear friend Colin when he moved to Australia. As we began to get to know each other, we also began to share our families. Susan and Martha (my life partner since 1987) hit it off as two sisters; both finding warmth and joy in each other's company.

My son Suheil got encouragement from Colin Uncle in his pursuits of cricket, including watching a game together in Delhi.

My daughter Tariqa enjoyed very much being part of the 'first family' in the wedding procession of Colin Uncle and Susan Aunty through the streets of Cuckfield in the summer of 2002.

Our family spent the Christmas in Australia with Susan, Colin and Anna in 2005. It was special, a moment of great joy and togetherness. Anna was full of her usual spirits, and even humming some Christmas carols.

We all were saddened when she became ill and hoped that it was a one-off episode. Anna bounced back in her true spirited form and never ceased to amaze everyone by her resilience, determination and love of life.

As Anna left this physical world in April this year, my life partner, and mother of my two children, and my professional colleague and strength, Martha also left this physical world in a shocking manner a month later.

Anna and Martha have carried on their life's journeys through the spirit world; their life spirits are vibrant, joyous and generous.

We are remembering their gifts and smiles today so that we can carry forward that life spirit in the next phase of our journeys ahead.

Thank you Anna, thank you Martha!

Dr Rajesh Tandon
President
UNESCO Chair in community based research and
social responsibility in higher education
August 2015

About the Author

Susan was born in Brisbane and has lived in the United Kingdom and Italy. She lives life to the fullest! Her passion is to make a difference to the quality of life of people with disabilities. However, she now sees this scope as much broader and wishes to share *Universal Life Lessons from My Brilliant Blue Bohemian Butterfly*, a book full of lessons that will enable us all to not only accept our differences, but embrace them.

Susan has been involved in the community sector for over thirty years. She has been an advocate for her daughter, Anna, and many others in need through her dedicated service to others. She is a founding member of National Disability Practitioners and a fully qualified disability support worker with training and assessment expertise. Susan completed her Information, Advice and Guidance qualification in the United Kingdom. She is also accredited in the art of hosting where she brings people together who can contribute to the conversation and find solutions to improve their quality of life.

She is a member of Chromosome 22 Central, a support group for families and individuals with disorders of chromosome 22, and also of the Velocardiofacial Syndrome 22q11 Foundation, which is a not-for-profit support and awareness group.

Susan's other passions include her love of art. She has had two exhibitions in the past few years displaying her photography and also her paintings, which she has absolutely loved creating. They bring out her creativity and enable her to bring balance to her life, and through these exhibitions she is able to give generous donations to her charities of choice. *Art of Giving*, which is the name of her artistic ventures, reflects her approach to life in whatever she does.

She is currently on the Board of Access Arts Incorporated and Paint Your Life Foundation, and is a founding member and youth director of the Rotary Club of New Farm. Susan is a public speaker with a focus on honouring our loved ones from birth to death. She is also a volunteer community correspondent for 612 ABC.

Susan is a global leader presenting Universal Life Lessons Workshops around the world to a broad range of groups in areas such as early intervention, youth, transition, careers advice, disability, aged care, end-of-life, and bereavement support.

As a life coach, Susan is also able to provide individual information, advice, and guidance sessions.

For more information please visit
www.universallifelessons.com

Anna Rose Paas

'Susan has authored a moving and inspiring account of the amazing life of her recently passed daughter, Anna Rose Paas.

I count myself as very fortunate to be able to come to know Anna while she was here. Susan's account shines a revealing light on Anna's life and is imbued with the deep love and commitment that Susan devoted to Anna for all of her twenty-nine short years.

If you want some inspiration and some insight into the rich life that someone with quite profound disability can experience, you must read this book.'

David Thompson AM
CEO, Jobs Australia

www.ingramcontent.com/pod-product-compliance
Lightning Source LLC
Chambersburg PA
CBHW071330190426
43193CB00041B/1128